*To Carolyn,*
*With admiration,*
*Liz*

# raising
# huck
# & ted

## a mother's guide to parenting

## LIZ PARSONS

**Health Communications, Inc.**
**Deerfield Beach, Florida**

*www.hcibooks.com*

**Library of Congress Cataloging-in-Publication Data**

Parsons, Liz.
  Raising Huck and Ted : a mother's guide to parenting / Liz Parsons.
    pages cm
  ISBN 978-0-7573-1802-3 (Paperback)
  ISBN 0-7573-1802-9 (Paperback)
  ISBN 978-0-7573-1751-4 (ePub)
  ISBN 0-7573-1751-0 (ePub)
  1. Motherhood.   2. Parenting   3. Mother and child.   I. Title.
  HQ759.P2875 2013
  306.874'3—dc23

                          2013035716

Publisher: Health Communications, Inc.
              3201 S.W. 15th Street
              Deerfield Beach, FL 33442–8190

*Cover design by Dane Wesolko*
*Inside design and formatting by Dawn Von Strolley Grove*

*In memory of my mom,*

*the only other person who ever picked my nose*

# Contents

# Introduction

HUCK AND TED ARE BRAVE, RESOURCEFUL, AND *FICTIONAL* BOYS. They materialized one evening at bedtime when our sons Ted and Marshall were young.

"Would you like me to tell you a story?" my husband Steve asked our boys and that's when Huck and Ted were born. Steve chose the names at random but it was understood that Marshall, our younger son, was Huck and Ted was—well, Ted. Night after night Steve drew out the adventure story, weaving aspects of Ted and Marshall's daily life into the fabric of the tale.

Huck and Ted faced epic challenges of Steve's making. There were wrongs to be righted and evils to overcome. The two boys joined forces, and relying on courage, humor, and ingenuity they resolved conflict and reestablished harmony.

Over the years those make-believe boys, Huck and Ted, have come to life in our sons. Like the bedtime story boys, Ted and Marshall have turned out well. So it may seem odd that I have never told either son that I am proud of him. People have strongly suggested it—nearly *insisted* on it. "You must be so proud of those boys," friends have said over the years. But I don't say that and our sons understand why.

I only know how to take pride in something I have worked at and accomplished myself. I *have* worked hard at being a good parent and a good role model. Well, most of the time. Sometimes I've succeeded: providing opportunities for our boys to learn and grow, holding them to the expectation of being the best Ted and the best Marshall they could be, and even the simple chore of making nutritious meals . . . of these things, I am proud.

But when our sons have been complimented on their work ethic or their ability to infuse fun into the workplace, when they have fought their way back from a critical illness, when they have worked without complaint or taken a stand for what they believe, this is what I've told them: "I am in awe of you. You have earned my deepest admiration and respect. I look to you as an example of how I might live my life. For the choices you make, the responsibility you take for the outcomes, and all the rewards you have reaped, *you* should feel so proud."

I love being their mom, and I dedicate these stories to them.

# CHAPTER 1

## *Welcome, Earthlings*

BEING PREGNANT WAS NOT MY FAVORITE THING—NOT BECAUSE OF getting fat, although that wasn't my favorite thing either, given that "maternity fashion" in those times was a complete oxymoron. I was over-the-moon excited about having a baby; it was just the *how* of it that creeped me out. I felt drawn into an alien experience that could not have been more bizarre.

The good news? You get to have a baby. The even better news? How you get to *make* the baby. But guess where the microscopic seedling is going to develop and grow? *Inside your body!* Then, after it has stretched your skin and poked and prodded all the places previously occupied by your own tissue and organs and bones, after it reaches its full width and length and heft—guess where it wants to come out? I'd have been better suited if I'd been a chicken or a robin, loyally content to sit on my offspring until they hatched.

I wasn't much of a baby person, either. Definitely, not one of the naturals. I recall sitting in the chair in our hospital room holding our firstborn. He was all wrapped up in a little blue bunny rug. The morning shift of the nursing staff had just come on the floor, and we hadn't met yet; this baby boy had been delivered just before midnight. A pretty young nurse stopped to admire the new addition. "What's his name?" she asked.

There was a painfully long silence until I realized she was talking to *me*. All I could think as I looked into her lovely, inquisitive face was, *How am I supposed to know? I just met him, too.* And that's the look I gave her.

Realizing she was waiting for an answer, I filed through the options we'd discussed. Sam? No. But we'd come close to choosing that. I looked at the small face. Ted. That's who he was. It seemed suddenly very arbitrary, but apparently this was Ted.

It wasn't that I didn't love our babies, because I did. I liked how they both smelled like warm biscuits. Actually, there were lots of things I loved about them; it was only that much of the time I couldn't understand them or what to *do* with them.

My sister, Nancy—now there's a baby person for you—seemed to understand them. "I don't know what else to do!" I complained to her as Ted wailed in the background.

"Put him down for a nap," she instructed me. "He's just tired."

"How do you know he's tired?" I demanded.

"Because that's a tired-baby cry," she told me. In about

the same tone of voice she'd have used to tell me where eggs come from. Like it was something everybody knew.

I looked at her blankly. "What do you mean a *tired* cry?" I asked.

My sister shrugged. "Babies have very different cries; there's one for when they're hungry, one for when they're tired, and one for when they have gas pains. They're all distinctive. *That* is the sound of a tired baby."

I listened intently, training my ear to pick up this nuance. "Nope, it just sounds like crying to me," I told her, now certain I was not a natural.

But I suspect my sister is right. These newest earthlings arrive with a language all their own. They also come so wonderfully packaged, with all the remaining characteristics of people: little fingernails and tiny whorled ears, exquisitely small insteps, and filaments as eyelashes. I used to sit and stare into their miniature faces as they nursed and wonder, *Who* are *you?*

At the same time, I was wondering when we could be finished with the whole nursing thing. I'm a great proponent of breast-feeding, and I'm always the first to recommend it as healthy and convenient (unless you'd hoped to ever sleep through the night again) and a beautiful experience (if you ignore the breast pads), but I'd never asked for big boobs, and certainly not ones that *leaked*.

In the months we awaited the arrival of our second child, I fretted, knowing I would soon be reentering alien territory. Where would this new baby fit in? Three of us had already created a complete family portrait. Where would a fourth get wedged in?

"Tell me again," I entreated Steve, my hand on my growing belly. I reached for my hair dryer as Ted played at my feet. Steve, now dressed, was exiting the bathroom. "Where will this baby be in this picture?"

As he always did, Steve smiled and squeezed me tight. "You'll see," he said, leaving me still wondering.

He was right, of course. The day Marshall was born, my heart grew bigger—much, much bigger, just as Dr. Seuss had assured us it could. And so did my life.

And even though I'd never believed in love at first sight, I witnessed it right there, in that hospital room. Steve brought Ted in to meet his new brother. We snugged his almost three-year-old frame into the only chair in the room, placed a pillow on his lap, and laid his downy-haired sibling on his lap.

I can see it in the photo we took at that moment—captured on film and played out for all the years since their brotherly adventure began—a love that continues to defy any boundaries I thought existed.

I look at that picture sometimes and think how lucky we were that those two little boys were visited on us, just as Dr. Seuss described: Thing 1 and Thing 2.

Miraculous.

## ᙎ What Every Child Wants

Before Steve and I started our family, we went to our family practitioner, Dr. John Jacono, to ask what we needed to know. That caught the doc a little off guard, given the fairly advanced ages we'd reached when hoping to become parents. "Exactly where do you need me to start?" he asked, his eyebrows perched high on his forehead. Relieved that we knew the mechanics, he moved on to a list of recommendations, like taking folic acid supplements. At the point Steve and I thought the appointment had reached its conclusion, we started to stand up.

"Do you know what it is you can give your child that every child wants?" The doc's question stopped us, squatting over our chairs.

Steve and I exchanged blank looks, having come quite unprepared for a quiz.

"Happy parents," he told us. "More than anything else, children want happy parents."

It continues to be the most significant piece of advice we've ever received.

## ᙎ Get Advice from Those Who Know

Here I'm passing on the next most important advice I was given: read Barbara Coloroso's book *Kids Are Worth It*. In fact, read anything she has written, even if it's scrawled on a cocktail napkin. And go wherever you have to in order to hear her speak. I did—more than once—and came away heartened and inspired. What I could never figure out was how a woman with such a full life and busy schedule had the energy to think and talk as fast as she does. I've always appreciated having been steered in her direction.

I also joined a neighborhood parenting group that met weekly at our local elementary school for a term. I picked up some good advice there from parents who were ahead of me on the experience curve. I subscribed to, and read, parenting magazines. In all, I tried to stay educated. Whenever I got discouraged, I'd remember the motto for our local kennel club: TAKE YOUR DOG TO OBEDIENCE SCHOOL; YOU'LL BOTH LEARN A LOT. It seemed to sum up the process of equipping myself for being an effective, loving parent.

## ⚘ Practical Tips

I had the good fortune of not only having a nurse for a sister but also having nurses as next-door neighbors— in two cities. And I have a friend who is a pediatrician. These women provided very practical answers to my desperate calls for help. They instructed me on how to treat cradle cap, how to suction boogers from a baby's nose, how to roll a baby's knees gently into his tummy to (hopefully) push the gas out and, more hopefully, stop the crying. They told me when to go to the emergency room. In return, I told them that if their children ever needed help with phonics, to be sure to call me—any time, night or day. A career in teaching does not prepare you for babies.

## ❦ Baby Nails

The best time to cut babies' nails is when they're asleep, and the best tool is your own front teeth—or even better, just peel a tiny crescent off with your own fingernail after their bath, while their nails are especially soft. This was much better advice than what I was attempting with a sharp tool and no experience.

Another tip: If your baby's big toe starts to look inflamed, as though the toenail is pushing into the flesh alongside the nail, cut a tiny V-shaped notch in the top edge of the nail with nail scissors. This will reduce the pressure caused by the expanding width of the nail into the soft tissue.

## ❦ Baby Teeth

Running the back of a little spoon over your baby's gums will announce the arrival of a new tooth with the smallest of clinks, long before your finger can feel the ridge.

## ❦ Baby Grease

At bath time, unclench your newborn baby's fists enough to wash the tiny palms and between the fingers. Be equally attentive to those pudgy folds of flesh under the chin. The greasy white coating called vernix that is on babies at birth collects in those places, and after a week or so it makes them smell like something other than biscuits. I know.

## ❦ Celebrate!

From my friend Sue, I learned the importance of celebrating and that it's easier than I thought. Don't hold out for a report card of straight As, or the high school graduation ceremony or the long-awaited first job. Get out the balloons, hang the streamers, and pop the sparkling cider the first time your kid gets an adult tooth, prints his or her name, jumps into the swimming pool, or rides a two-wheeler. Never delay joy.

## ❦ Spread the Joy

For a while we had a neighbor who used to say to us each year, as we packed our bags for a November holiday in the sun, "I hope it rains the entire time you're there." Perhaps she thought that was funny, but it felt mean-spirited. Demonstrate to your children the gift of rejoicing in other people's successes and joy. It's like multiplying happiness.

## ᴪ Baby Food

I didn't like baby food. Anything other than strained fruit made me gag—even the little bit I put on my lip to test the temperature. I had to wipe it off with a tissue because I certainly wasn't going to lick it off. So when our boys were ready to eat mushed-up meats and vegetables, my doctor friend taught me how to make my own baby food with things like chicken, broccoli, and potatoes and a hand-held food processor. I am forever grateful.

## ᴪ Snug as a Bug in a Rug

There's another tidbit I remember, but it didn't come from a nurse; it came from my friend who's of Greek and Italian descent. She runs a busy family-style restaurant and a busy family. I stopped in to visit her one day at her diner. I wanted to show off our new baby boy. After the car ride, Ted was, for the most part, asleep. That seemed ideal to me; Teresa could admire our sleeping baby, and she and I could chat and drink good coffee. I set the baby seat on the bench beside me hoping Ted would continue to sleep, but he wouldn't stay settled. His tiny arms kept snapping up in the air, startling him awake, and I couldn't figure out why.

"Do you have a little blanket?" Teresa asked me. It was mid-August and stinking hot outside. I had a clean cloth diaper I kept on hand for wiping up little messes. Carefully, Teresa draped the open cotton sheet over the baby seat and tucked the edges lightly around Ted's small body. Instantly, his whole form relaxed, and he fell into a sound sleep.

I remember looking at Teresa and asking, "Why'd you do that?"

"Think of what it's like if you're drifting off to sleep on the sofa and someone comes and covers you with a blanket. Don't you love how it makes you feel so cozy and secure? Same thing for babies," she shrugged. As if that too was something everybody would know.

## ❦ Island Babies

Steve and I had decided we wanted to have just two kids, and we were careful to ensure that outcome. By some odd coincidence, both boys turned out to be island babies. Ted was conceived on Tasmania—we're fairly sure it was in the hotel in Hobart with the room that looked like a turn-of-the-last-century brothel. Marshall began on Prince Edward Island, where our cottage bed squeaked in the room next to Ted's, creating interesting challenges.

After we had weaned Marshall at the age of six months, Steve and I took a sweetheart holiday to New York City. We walked and dined and laughed. Later at night, in our Manhattan hotel, Steve pulled me close in bed and whispered in my ear, "You know, we're on an island." How could he have known that "oral" contraception would mean a poorly timed sentence?

## 🌱 Who Are You?

Throughout the years, continue to look at your children and wonder, *Who are you?* Discovering the answer is what this great adventure is all about. It's how I came to recognize Huck and Ted in our boys.

# CHAPTER 2

## *Meet Lambie*

I REMEMBER THE DAY WE MET WOODY. TED WAS ABOUT TO TURN five, and Marshall was two. I'd called a breeder and said our family wanted a Labrador retriever puppy, and asked if could we come and see if we liked any of the ones they had for sale. She said, nicely, that we could come; they had one pup left. But, she explained that our two-hour drive would be so she and her husband could meet us. Then *they* would decide if they liked us well enough to *let* us buy one of their puppies.

Properly humbled, we agreed, and the four of us piled into the car. Approaching the farmhouse, I was stricken with a sudden nervousness. Turning to Steve, and not wanting to waken Ted and Marshall, who had nodded off in the backseat, I whispered, "What if we don't *like* this puppy? What if the reason it's the last one is because it's not cute? Then what do we do? What do we tell the boys?"

Slowing the car to turn up the lane, Steve turned to me and said, deadpan, "When have you ever met a puppy you didn't like?"

That was the day Woody joined our family.

Being a retriever, he loved to carry things around in his mouth. He would return from foraging in the neighborhood with a small black patent-leather shoe or a man's soft leather glove held gently in his jaw like a duckling, and after wiping off the dog spit, I would have to canvas the homes on our street, red-faced, to return these things to their rightful owners.

Not everything Woody brought home was returnable, though. One very special May afternoon, he climbed the stairs to our back deck after an excursion to the fields beyond our fence, walked to where I sat enjoying the sunshine, and dropped a desiccated mouse corpse at my toes. Happy Mother's Day.

But this natural tendency to retrieve is what made it so easy for Woody to learn to clear his dish. That and the fact a Lab will do *anything* for food.

We had decided that when each of our boys turned four, he was old enough to clear his own plate, so when it was Marshall's turn, we began the routine after every meal.

"Clear your dish," I would say. "Bring it to the kitchen." Over and over, watching for the day Marshall would automatically pick up his plate after (1) asking to be excused, and (2) saying thank you to the cook.

We taught the boys to say, "Good breakfast, Mom. We love you, Mom. You're a babe, Mom." Or alternatively,

"Good dinner, Dad. We love you, Dad. You're a stud, Dad." We'd borrowed these lines from friends who were trying to teach their kids manners, too. It was fun, done in a sing-songy voice—a little wacky, but it got the message across.

On about day five, things were coming along nicely with Marshall—what with him needing fewer and fewer reminders. But after breakfast I caught him walking away from the table empty-handed. "Hey, you," I called out, "go get your dish and bring it to the kitchen."

Woody looked at me with the light bulb expression I'd come to recognize, walked to his empty metal bowl at the far side of the breakfast nook, and stuck his foot in it, flipping it up on its edge. He picked it up in his teeth, brought it to the kitchen, and dropped it with a loud clang at my feet. I laughed out loud and then gave him a biscuit.

That was the end of our plate-clearing training sessions. Woody cleared his dish after every meal until he was fifteen, rewarded with more than his weight in Milkbones. And at fifteen, Marshall was doing an equally good job.

Woody did more than just carry stuff around in his mouth, however. He used to chew things, too. The pliable plastic that play figures are made of was particularly appealing to him.

We had an extensive collection of miniature Disney movie characters: the Little Mermaid, Belle and the Beast, Simba, Peter Pan, the Lady and the Tramp, and a large litter of Dalmatians—pretty much the entire 101 cast. We kept them in a stacker basket on a play table with other toys. But that's not where the boys played with them. They liked to put them on floor level, where none of the toys stood a chance.

Thanks to Woody, Captain Hook was missing a hand. That's to be expected, but in our collection, Cinderella's arm ended at her elbow and Prince Charming was minus a foot. It was like a hospital ward for amputees. Five of the seven dwarfs, Tinkerbell, and Aladdin were double amputees. The ones who got decapitated we threw out; those with only puncture wounds were considered lucky.

But that wasn't the worst of it. What Woody really loved to do was chew the ears off plush toys. He transformed every teddy bear we put in his basket into the image of a baby seal. He even figured out how to leave the antlers while eating the ears off the stuffed reindeer Santa left for him.

Eventually, we settled on buying him a succession of furry hedgehogs that honked when he bopped them on the floor (hedgehogs being earless to the naked eye). In doing so, we hoped the dog would forget his destructive fetish.

Now let me introduce Lambie—*Precious* Lambie, to

be precise. She would belong to Ted, given to him as a newborn by a much-loved cousin. Where Ted has gone, so has Lambie: preschool, kindergarten, family camp. When Ted got chicken pox; so did Lambie—little contagious red French knots stitched with thread while Ted slept. As Ted's rash spread, so did Lambie's—more vivid pox appeared against her pastel plaid each morning. Then, as Ted recovered, Lambie's spots were carefully plucked out, again while Ted slept, until, miraculously, the two of them recovered simultaneously.

Imagine the day Woody appeared in the family room with Lambie in his jaws, looking forlorn. Actually, he looked guilty. Lambie looked forlorn.

To his credit, some sense of loyalty must have kicked in before Woody devoured any body parts, but Lambie's left ear had a ragged tear.

Ted was distraught. We sat together on the sofa and assessed the damage. A sizable patch of limp woven plaid hung in a flap. Thankfully, I noticed that the shiny pink satin of her inner ear was still intact.

I thought I remembered Lambie's lineage to be out of Hasbro Toys, but the chances of there being a clone of her, or even a descendant, on a shelf anywhere on the continent were long gone. Not that I was considering *replacing* Precious Lambie—hush! I was thinking about an organ donor.

"Well, Ted," I said softly, cuddling him closer and thinking fast, "what's happened to Lambie is like when a kid has an accident—maybe falling off a bicycle or cutting a finger on something really sharp. When that happens to people, we go to the hospital, and a doctor sews us back up. So the good news is Lambie can be fixed."

Ted looked up at me, his lower lip quivering. "But I *never* wanted Lambie to get hurt." His voice caught in his throat. "And I never wanted her to get *stitches!*"

I told him I felt the same way about him and about Marshall. That I never wanted them to have to get stitches. But if the day ever came when that's what they needed, that's what we'd do. I also knew that if that day ever arrived, I'd go looking for the best doctor I could find. So that's what we did for Lambie.

Because, stitching those little red chicken pox French knots was about the limit of my expertise with a needle and thread, and I only knew how to make them because I'd seen a how-to diagram once. To say I'm not a seamstress would make people who truly know me laugh.

In the autumn of ninth grade (or Grade Nine as we say in Canada), when I was fourteen and miniskirts were new, I had to sew an apron in home economics class—cross-stitched, with handy pockets, no less, and little embroidery floss xxx's everywhere. A pattern of tiny crosses had to match exactly the pattern of little xxx's on the aprons my girlfriends were making. We could choose our gingham: pink or green or orange or—who cared?! The only idea more ludicrous than us making an apron was the idea any of us would wear one. I chose red.

Our next assignment was knitting. I knew my home economics days were over. Long before the advent of high-tech fabrics that repel moisture and keep hands warm and dry, everybody's mittens were knitted. When the temperature hit 23°F (-5°C), we'd wear one pair over another. When it hit 14°F (-10°C), we'd breathe out all our warm air in a long exhalation through the wool to thaw our freezing fingertips. This caused icing. The outside mitten would get all balled up with snow and crusty frost that we could pull off with our teeth, leaving us to spit out the fuzz. Coming in from outdoors, we'd pull the pairs apart and lay them on top of a hot radiator. As the heat hit, they'd give off the musky aroma of a flock of wet sheep.

In early November that year, it was my good fortune that an entire basket of freshly knitted mittens, in every possible size and color, linked together with a single fine loop of coordinating yarn, had just been delivered to my mother by the woman she'd paid to knit them. My sisters and brothers and I would wear and lose them throughout the season. I chose a medium-sized black pair and handed them in to my home economics teacher. I got an A+ in knitting.

On the sofa with Ted, Lambie in hand, I could tell some form of home economics stitchery, whether with thread or yarn, would be required to close her gaping wound. I could also tell from Ted's expectant, trusting expression that he was looking to me to do something. After all, that's what we always say in our family: if something goes wrong, we'll all work together to make it right. That's how we ended up at Cheeseworth's.

We lived in Waterloo, Ontario—about an hour west of Toronto. We had plans to drive in to Toronto that weekend anyway, and Cheeseworth Invisible Mending wasn't far out of our way. Cheeseworth's was listed in Toronto Life magazine as *the* place to go in the city if you needed repairs made to a toy lamb. Well, not in those words exactly. To me it seemed the ideal solution: Ted would witness our commitment to finding the very best care for his beloved stuffy, and we could just drop Lambie off, go do our errands, and pick her up on our way out of town. It was a simple outpatient procedure—she'd be just like new . . . but, apparently, not on a Saturday.

Standing at the curb outside Cheeseworth's, I gave Ted the information the nice woman behind the counter had given me: we could leave Lambie with her for the invisible menders to repair when they came back to work next week, then they'd put her in a box and mail her back to us.

As the words were coming out of my mouth, I knew that wasn't going to happen. "Leave Lambie in *Toronto*?!" Ted went pale. I don't think we'd ever characterized the city as a wild and dangerous place, but clearly Ted had formed his own opinion. He would not be leaving Precious Lambie behind—and certainly not with strangers! I never even got to the part about putting Lambie in a box.

"Or," I said, already dreading the idea that was formulating in my head, "we can take Lambie home with us, and *I'll* fix her."

There was only the briefest pause while Ted considered his options. His gaze moved from me to Lambie to the storefront at Cheeseworth's and back to me. For a moment I hoped he would turn down my offer. I even thought seriously about using the opportunity to tell him about the apron—and the mittens. But I didn't.

And so, when we arrived home, I sat with Ted again, and using the whipstitch I recalled from that how-to chart, I started the work. It took a lot of courage, though. *What if I make things worse?* A wave of panic rose as I pulled the first suture, then the next, through the fabric.

It was the look on Ted's face that did it for me: relief, to be sure—he'd have precious Lambie tucked in beside him that night. But it was even more than that, beyond gratitude—faith.

I'm glad about how it all turned out. Lambie's ear was restored to its original shape, although you can still see the scar—a meandering ridge of raised, pale blue, uneven stitches. Ted got over the fact that his dog was the perpetrator, and I learned a life lesson.

Fixing Lambie's ear was not about me, my fears, or my abilities; it was about Ted. As much as I fussed and stewed about how it would all turn out, it was never about embroidery, either. What I learned, in simply trying my best, was that although I exposed myself to be just like Lambie—flawed and imperfect—it didn't seem to matter to Ted.

## ❦ How to Eat Grapes

My mother-in-law gave us a pair of decorative grape scissors. She wanted her grandsons to know that when a large bunch of grapes is set out, it is good manners to snip off a small stem of them for yourself rather than picking individual grapes off and leaving the bunch looking plucked for the next diner. No scissors? Tear a small stem off with your fingers and put it on your plate. Eat from that portion. That's proper etiquette.

When she wasn't around, though, we'd have crazy grape-throwing contests from those personal-size portions. It's hard to sit still with your mouth open wide as somebody across the table uses it for target practice, but that's what we did. We'd also just toss the little orbs straight up in the air and try to catch them in own mouths. Both contests created a lot of laughs. We knew all about the choking risks; what we didn't know was that dogs should *not* eat grapes. Apparently eating too many is toxic to their systems. Woody must have had a strong constitution. He got more than his share of the fruit on account of not all of us being great shots but he never got sick—at least not from grapes.

## ❦ Miss Manners

A childless friend of mine gave us a Miss Manners book as a baby gift when Marshall was born. I wasn't sure I appreciated it—my postpartum hormones making me more than just a little touchy as they did—but I read it cover to cover and learned lots of niceties to pass along to our sons. I've actually seen them implement some of what they were taught, like going first through a set of revolving doors: moving those doors from a standstill takes some effort, and it's a small kindness to get the momentum going for the next person, who then glides through. When they were old enough, I left Miss Manners in their bathroom as reading material. Steve just laughed.

## ⚘ Sharing Meals

Teaching etiquette to your kids frees them to enjoy their time at dinner tables around the block and around the world. It's a process, so while you're at it, eat meals together and have fun. Ask, "What was the best part of your day? What was the worst?" And tell them about yours. Well, unless you got fired or backed your station wagon out of the garage right into your partner's new car, causing thousands of dollars' damage. Which I have done. At dinner that night, I said it was the worst part of my day. It wasn't. What I said on impact, with Marshall in the passenger seat to hear, was.

## ⚜ Teach Chores Early

Set the table for each meal unless it's toast and juice at the breakfast bar or a picnic on the floor, which is also fun. Better yet, teach your children to set the table. Use place mats and napkins. Make daily chores for your little ones routine and fun, and start early. (By that I mean both at a young age *and* first thing in the morning.)

Get the kids to put their plates and cups in the sink or load them into the dishwasher after the meal. Remove all the dangerously sharp items from the cutlery basket of the dishwasher or the dish rack in the sink, and have them put knives, forks, and spoons into the corresponding dividers in the kitchen drawer. It teaches them matching and sorting—and pitching in. (This works with finding pairs of socks from the laundry basket, too.) While they're at it, you can teach them what each utensil is used for.

Use unbreakables for the first few years, if need be. If you're too fussy about where things go in that appliance to allow toddlers to participate, get over it. Kids can learn to arrange things the way you like later; but get the habit established early. Remind yourself of my friend's advice: Everything goes *into* a dishwasher. You get to use, again, the things that come out.

## ᵂ Eating Out

Take your children out to eat, when you are able, as a reward for showing good manners at home. Choose a place where you don't have to line up at a counter and carry your own meal to a table. Give your children advance notice that the expectation is for them to put their good manners to use. That means stay seated and use an indoor voice.

Go prepared, knowing that kids are not wired for sitting nicely and waiting for the server to arrive with menus, then waiting longer for the food to show up. Keep in mind that other patrons may not think a loud, unruly tot is as adorable as you do. Have with you tools for quiet distraction. A child's lunch pail packed with age-appropriate items used only on special occasions is all you need. Fill it with things like small puzzles, crayons and a coloring book, pencils and paper for playing hangman or tic-tac-toe with you, finger puppets, colorful beads, and a string to make a necklace for Grandma.

Keep it out of kiddies' reach at home so the novelty of the playthings doesn't wear off, but store it where it's easy to grab on your way out the door. As you head out, consider adding a little tub of dry cereal, biscuits, or fruit to fill the gap till the meal arrives and a sippy cup to avoid spills. Allow every child his or her own kit. Remember to add and alternate new items regularly to hold your children's interest. Giving them something purposeful to do will take the stress off you, because they aren't able to just sit and be quiet. At least not for very long.

## ⚘ Teaching Good Behavior

Remember; children need your help in learning appropriate behaviors. Often it is a good idea to outline your expectations in advance when you're going someplace good manners are going to matter. And be specific—no murky generalizations. I learned that lesson the day I had an enlightening exchange with our four-year-old. I was tired and frustrated by whatever Ted was doing, so I'm pretty sure the instruction "Ted, I just want you to *be-have!*" came out as a growl. He looked up at me, confused and sad. "But, Mommy," he said, "I *am* being *have!*"

## ⚘ Coloring Books

Coloring books have their place in a child's learning, despite what some naysayers may warn. As kids advance from staying inside the lines, they come to recognize continuity of fields within an image. Think of a bunny peeking out from behind a tree; the child will come to recognize which enclosed areas belong to the tree in the foreground and which spaces to the left and right of it make up the bunny. It gets even more complicated when clothing, for instance, is added to the picture. As your children choose colors for pants or shirts, they learn to be on the lookout for bits of clothing that belong to the main piece but may be separated from it in the image by another element.

## Eat in Peace

There will always be times when points of conflict, discipline, and course corrections need to be discussed. As much as possible, do not choose to have these stressful conversations over a meal. Like the now outdated rule for safe swimming, wait an hour till your meal has digested before you dive into those waters. Everyone will feel better—and safer.

## Lunch Dates

Arrange the occasional lunch date with your kids— one parent taking one child somewhere special. This is particularly rewarding for a child who has recently welcomed (or not) a new sibling into the family. It puts the spotlight back on the elder child, at a time when he or she may be wondering why it shifted away in the first place.

## ☙ A Fun and Useful Game

Whether you're still waiting for the chicken nuggets to arrive or just sitting together around the table at home, here's a game for family and guests to play. We made it up and called it Yes, Yes, No. It teaches awareness, increases memory, and introduces the math concepts of sets and variables. The more people there are at the table, the harder it gets.

The object of the game is to figure out which observable characteristic or possession results in people at the table being sorted into one group or another.

One person begins by choosing an observable identifier without saying out loud what that identifier is. Then he or she points to each person, going around the table, including him- or herself, and labeling each person as yes (having that identifiable characteristic or possession) or no (not having it).

There may be any number of yeses or noes. For instance, at our table, the game once went yes, yes, no, no; the winner was the person who figured out that the identifier was eyeglasses. (Steve and Ted were wearing them, and Marshall and I weren't.)

The identifier could be who's drinking milk, who's wearing long pants, who's wearing a watch, who parts his or her hair, who has brown eyes, who's wearing a shirt that has buttons, or who has painted fingernails.

It can be anything observable.

A guess can often seem correct but turn out not to be the right answer. Soften the blow by telling the guesser, "That is absolu-u-u-tely wrong, but it's a fantastic observation and very clever of you," or, "That's so smart I wish I'd thought of it. But I didn't."

The person to guess correctly creates the next game. If no one can guess and everyone gives up, the person who stumped the group gets to go again. We did, however, make a house rule that if the person who created a game made it *impossible* to solve, the rest of us could give her or him the "raspberry," and the next turn would go to whoever came up with a next identifier the fastest.

Start by making it easy, and remember, even as it gets more difficult, everyone has to be able to see what it is that characterizes the group, because the real object of the game is to create winners all around.

This game became a very useful tool at our table when we wanted our boys to learn to put their napkins on their laps as soon as they sat down. We turned the challenge into a Yes, Yes, No contest; those of us who remembered would surreptitiously slide our napkins off the edge of the table and unfold them quietly, then wait to see who'd forget. "Yes, yes, yes, no." Just the sound of that pattern would result in a "D'oh!" from the violator. It became a joke among us, took away the pressure of parental nagging, and achieved the desired result through family fun.

## That's Not Funny

We have a family rule: something is only a joke if both people are laughing. That's what we reminded our boys when one hurt the other's feelings and then defended his actions by saying, "It was only a joke." It is essential for kids (and adults) to learn the difference. Whether coming from children or grown-ups, teasing tends to be mean. Sarcasm *is* mean. You'll know something was a joke if everybody's laughing.

## Creating a Safe Space

Your home is the one place you can create a sanctuary for every family member, safe from derision, name-calling, or worse. Make it everyone's responsibility to protect the others. One day I caught Ted being rough with Marshall. It had something to do with him grabbing at a toy he wanted. I intervened immediately, stepping between the boys. "I won't let you hurt Marshall," I told Ted. "This is his home. He has every right to be protected from being hurt in this house. I will protect him the same way I would protect you if someone tried to hurt *you*."

Our efforts to create a safe haven extended to our

guests. My mother used to call herself stupid. "I'm just so stupid," she'd agonize over some little misstep. We made her abide by our rule when she visited—our house, our rule: nobody gets to call anybody stupid, and that includes self-recrimination. Forgetful? Fine. Demonstrating a lack of forethought? We all do that. But stupid? No, because we all need room to safely make and learn from mistakes. Like backing into your husband's car.

I actually did that. Marshall was in the passenger seat. We were chatting as I reversed out of our one car garage.

Steve had arrived home the previous evening from a week-long business trip. It had snowed all night and was still snowing. So — I'd say I didn't really see his car, but the truth is, I wasn't really looking.

# CHAPTER 3

## *Flushed with Pride*

"Come see what I made," Ted invited me.

I was curious to know what he'd produced after half an hour of quiet creativity. We'd picked up three giant boxes from the appliance store earlier that week: one for Ted, one for Marshall, and one in case a friend joined them for a playdate. We'd cut openings for windows and made hinged doors for privacy. For now, the boxes were aligned like a streetscape in our living room, the cushions from the sofa padding the interiors. That afternoon, as Marshall napped, I'd suggested that Ted take his box of crayons and decorate his house.

"What do you mean?" he asked.

"I don't know; you decide," I told him. "Some nice pictures on the walls, maybe, or just some designs. Something to cheer it up inside." *Something that takes a while*, I was thinking, as I lay down on the sofa in the family room for a little respite. Off went Ted.

But soon he was back, still looking puzzled.

"You mean draw with my crayons?"

"Yeah," I shrugged, nodding encouragingly.

"On the walls?"

"Yeah," I agreed again, and picked up my novel.

But he was still standing there. "You mean I can draw pictures on the walls of my house?"

"Sure," I told him. "It's your house; you can do what you want with it."

*Really?* He didn't actually say that, but I could tell it's what he was thinking. He searched my face for traces of kidding, then a flash of inspiration crossed his face, and he turned and left. I opened to my bookmark.

After a while he was back with the invitation. I swung my feet to the floor and stood up to follow him, excited. I've always loved kids' art, especially their first drawings of people. They look exactly like what a toddler sees from floor level as he or she gazes upward: two long, long legs that disappear into a giant head. And they hover above the ground as if still considering joining the life of a grounded human.

Across the family room, Ted had us turn left. We could have gone straight ahead, through the dining room to the living room, but this was his tour, and I wasn't in charge. So we went into the foyer, and again Ted turned left, into the laundry room. Just as concerns were forming questions in my head, Ted stepped into what I called the powder room—the main floor half bathroom. He turned, beaming with pride.

"See?" He stepped back to reveal his Crayola fresco.

A riot of color and story unraveled along one cream-colored wall, breached the corner, and continued on to the right, stopping only when it reached the toilet paper holder. Shocked into silence I took in the details frame by frame. There was a red house and a garden. Tulips and trees. And kids playing.

"Oh, Ted," I gasped, sinking down against the vanity to his level and pulling him close. He was studying my face again. "This is beautiful, but why would you draw on our bathroom walls?"

"Because you told me I could," he defended himself, nervously.

"Oh, Ted," I repeated, "I meant your *cardboard* house." And then I snorted. It was just too funny. I laughed, then Ted laughed, and for a while we just sat there, piled in on the powder room floor, laughing at what we had done.

Not long after, I made my next mistake: I repainted the powder room. I covered up the multihued story Ted had created with more cream-colored paint. I've always regretted that, because, truth be told, the cream-colored paint did nothing to cheer up our house inside.

Actually, other funny things happened in that powder room. Woody led me there another day to show me he'd dropped his rubber duck into the open toilet bowl. I don't think he took me to the scene out of remorse; it's my guess he thought it was funny, being a water dog and all. Surrounded by testosterone—whether junior, senior, or canine in origin—I didn't take me long to figure out that guys think bathroom material is hysterical.

"Come see what I made!" It was an echoed, excited invitation from one of our boys as I followed, yet again, through the laundry room, wondering, *What now?*

There, in the open toilet bowl, was—not a rubber duck—but the longest poo I'd ever seen. It was a source of enormous four-year-old male pride, something to be exhibited before being flushed.

That may have been the first time I rolled my eyes and declared, "I should have had girls!", but it wasn't the last. . . .

"Can we watch?" Marshall's question was directed at Steve. I remember sitting across the table from them, all those males in my life, stunned.

Dinner was half eaten and a game of Yes, Yes, No was well underway. I'd been surveying the family looking for the solution to the puzzle when, from the corner of my eye, I caught a flash of silver in the aquarium beside us. Not *in*, exactly. *On*. As in floating, belly side up. Startled, I screamed.

That, naturally, brought an end to the game and the meal. I was distressed; goldfish were our sons' first pets, and these particular ones had been with us for a long time. I'd never thought to prepare our boys for a moment like this.

Steve stood up, pushing his chair back. "I'll look after it," he volunteered. As if I might have.

"What are you going to do, Dad?" Marshall queried.

*What* are *you going to do?* I wondered silently.

"I'm going to scoop it out with the net and then I'm going to dispose of it." Steve's response was calm and level, and I wondered what, precisely, my hero meant by *dispose of.*

"How?" Apparently, Ted wanted to know, too.

"I'm going to flush it down the toilet." Steve told them.

I stared at my husband, slack-jawed and bug-eyed. Without using the word *barbarian*, I was trying to decide how I might guide him to offer a different, possibly more dignified, solemn end-of-life ceremony in this, our children's first exposure to death. Something that might involve a satin-lined jewelry box and a tiny grave marker.

I needn't have bothered. That's when Marshall piped up, filling the awkward gap, "Can we watch?"

The three of them headed happily to the powder room, and as I listened to their squeals of joy over the swish of water, I thought again, *I* should *have had girls*.

## ᴥ Sound Effects

I can't give all the credit to the males in my family for creating levity with bathroom humor, although they are perhaps more fond of it than I am. Steve bought a book for Ted and Marshall. It's like other books the boys have owned—there is a series of little buttons across the bottom and a miniature speaker embedded in the plastic panel. In earlier years, the books we purchased made the sounds of fire engines or ice cream trucks. This version, however, plays seven different fart sounds and gives colorful descriptions of each.

None of them seem as funny to me as the sound I made standing in the kitchen one day. Little Ted was beside me. I thought I could just squeak one out without him knowing, but the flatulence I passed came with its own sound effect.

Quite astonished, and with newfound admiration, Ted looked up and exclaimed, "Mom, you sound like a duck!"

## ᴥ Choose Pets Carefully

I probably should have foreseen the lack of sentimentality that pervaded the flushing ceremony for that little goldfish. The three flashy swimmers had been a surprise gift from Santa. Along with leaving the tank and the bubbler and an adequate supply of fish food, Santa had written a note for Ted, telling him the pets had not yet been named, so he could do the honors.

We waited a few days, then I prodded him, "Whatcha gonna call them, Ted?"

He turned his head ever so slightly and stared at me. "They're *fish*," he said.

Apparently, something that required a leash was more of what Ted had in mind, so when Marshall was nearly two and Ted four, Steve and I brought home an eighteen-month-old large, purebred herding-type dog that we named Solo. We had learned through a neighbor that a local breeder had gone bankrupt and could no longer afford to feed the animals left in his kennel. The dogs were facing the possibility of being put down, so they were being given away for free.

Within the first few days, the boys and I took Solo to the veterinarian for her healthy puppy checkup. The vet walked into the room, looked at the dog, looked at the boys, looked at me, and said, "Never leave the room and leave that dog alone with these children." That should have been enough of a clue.

Just weeks later, Solo got jealous. She'd adopted me as her favorite and didn't like the fact I was on the floor playing with Marshall. She walked up behind me and bit me hard enough on the back of my arm to make me yelp. Recalling the vet's clear warning, and grateful the dog had chosen to nip me and not Marshall, I stood and went immediately to the phone. "You will have to come and get Solo," I told the breeder. "She can't stay here."

Do not keep pets that endanger your children's safety. We had not done our homework in researching a breed of dog that would be suited to a home with young, active children. Of course we don't want our kids to think animals are expendable, but what lesson do we teach our children if we fail to protect them?

Solo was placed in a home with teenage children and lived a happy life there, terrorizing their cat. After considerable investigation, we decided to find a Labrador retriever puppy. That is how we came to welcome Woody into our family. He remained a treasured companion for just over fifteen years.

## Dealing with Death

It's a difficult time when our children encounter death. While Ted and Marshall were very young, their grandfather, Pops, died. Not long after, we lost their young aunt to cancer. In each case, we decided to include our boys in the observation of their relative's passing. When there were open caskets at visitation, we explained the tradition as an opportunity to say goodbye to the body in which we had come to know and love that person here on earth.

## ❦ Write Notes to Your Kids

Write to your kids: a thank-you note for helping out, a congratulatory note on what a good job they've done remembering to make their beds, or improving behavioral issues. Make tiny cards that they will find under their pillows or at their places at the table. Try to print in the style your children are taught at school (children do not print in all capital letters the way some adults do). If they're too young to read, read the note to them, or be creative and communicate as much of your message in picture form as you can. Display the note as a reminder of their accomplishment, maybe with a framed photo to attest to their new skill.

When our sons turned eighteen, I wrote them both a long letter—kind of a rite of passage into adulthood. When it was Ted's turn, he was working as a camp counselor, and our family didn't have the chance to be together on that day, so I mailed his letter to him. In it I asked Ted to stay in touch with that bold, brave boy who would take a set of crayons to a bland, blank wall. "Nurture that kid," I told him. "There is much he can teach us all."

## ❦ Teach Your Kids to Write

Having been an elementary school teacher, I was always encouraging our sons to write. Part of that was the ritual of annual letters to Santa. Now, even as grown young men, they still write to Santa with little urging. Each letter begins "Well, Sir, it's been quite a year." Reading the collection of those letters and Santa's responses provides us with a fairly comprehensive journal of our adventures and misadventures over the years.

Another idea is to have your kids write letters to themselves. At thirteen, as they enter the teen years, they can be challenged to compose a letter to themselves to be sealed and tucked away, to be opened only when they turn twenty and are leaving their teens behind. Have them list the things they hope they will have accomplished, the kind of people they hope to be, and what jobs they predict they will have held. If they are still listening to you, suggest they repeat the exercise on their twentieth birthday to be read when they turn thirty.

Remember to respect the boundaries of their privacy. Only read what they've written if you're invited to.

## ▼Help with the Light Switch

When our boys were old enough to get to the bathroom and get themselves up onto the toilet seat, they still weren't tall enough to reach the light switch. That meant they needed us to accompany them to the bathroom simply to flip the switch. Steve saved us many steps by installing an assisting device. At that time, it was a pair of little balls that hung on strings from a ring that operated the toggle. Pull the green ball down, and the light goes on; pull the red ball down, and the light goes off. We put them in the boys' bedrooms, too. Versions of these aids are still available.

## 🌷 A House Within A House

We had a homemade playhouse in the unfinished section of our very large basement. It was given to us when my sister's children outgrew it and was big enough for our boys to move around inside making pretend meals in the kitchen and setting the table for guests. It had real fiberboard walls taller than our sons, plus a door and window boxes, curtains, wallpaper, and pint-sized appliances. We stocked the cupboards with plastic food, cutlery, and plates. There was a tiny coffeemaker and a sink that pumped real water from a reservoir. We put cheap green carpet around the exterior to simulate a lawn. Then we added kid-size deck chairs, a tiny patio table, and a plastic lawn mower.

Ride-in toy cars, brought inside for winter, allowed the home's occupants to jump into them and drive around our furnace to the child-size gas pump or across the room to the grocery store, which was fully equipped with a shopping cart, a cash register, and play money. Kids used to come from all over the neighborhood to play there. Few stayed to help clean up.

Our family hosted a big reunion party one year. Almost twenty years later, one sister-in-law remembers that playhouse as the best thing she'd ever seen. Her kids loved it!

But after a comment I overheard my cousin Sarah make to her children the day of the reunion, I wondered whether we'd overdone the whole toy thing in the basement. Sarah was preparing her four kids to leave. I happened to pass behind her as she was whispering—well, more like hissing—at her children to get back down those stairs and help clean up the mess she'd seen in our basement.

"But, Mom," her daughter argued, "it was like that when we got here."

"Don't give me that nonsense," my cousin replied. "*Nobody's* basement looks like that!"

# CHAPTER 4

## *Can I Sleep with You?*

ONE OF THE MOST IMPORTANT THINGS I EVER TAUGHT OUR SONS TO say was "Dad? Dad—I had a bad dream."

"But more quietly," I instructed—so only Daddy can hear.

That's because I'm really not good when you wake me up. By *good*, I mean *nice*. I'm not nice when you wake me up.

I remember Ted arriving at our bedside in the dark, Lambie in a death grip under his armpit. "Mom. Mom? Mom!"

I awoke with a start, his small face almost touching mine.

"What?!" The annoyance was automatic and already beginning to build.

"I had a bad dream," he whispered, as though it were a secret.

"Well, it's all over now," I mumbled, and I pulled the covers back over my head. "Go back to bed."

"You did *not* say that!" my friend Bonnie gasped, practically inhaling her coffee when I told her.

"Yes, I did," I insisted. "I'm with these kids from six in

the morning till bedtime. I need some space to myself."
Besides, Steve and I had had the conversation about
co-sleeping and decided it wasn't for us. First, it didn't
feel safe. Second, when we're asleep, we both prefer to
abide by the "See this line? Don't cross it" rule. In other
words, "Don't touch me, I'm sleeping."

"But, Liz," she implored, "he's just a little kid."

Okay, I decided. I could take her point and work on
softening my position on midnight wake-up calls.

"Can I sleep with you tonight?" Ted was bathed and
in fresh pajamas. Story time was over, and Marshall was
in his crib. My hand was on the light switch when Ted
delivered the preemptive question.

Remembering my new resolution, I walked back and
sat on the edge of his bed. "No, Ted, this is your bed, and
this is where you sleep."

"But I don't want to sleep by myself," he whimpered. I
could see he was trying to be brave.

"You're not alone," I told him. "You have Lambie."

Ted looked furtively at Lambie, then leaned in closer
to me. "But she's not *real*," he whispered. "And, besides,"
he continued, "*you* get to sleep with somebody."

He had a point, and it almost made me laugh. "Tell you
what," I bargained for my solitude, "you go to sleep here
in your bed, and if you have a bad dream, you can come
and wake me."

And he did. This time I peeled back the blankets and pulled him up into our big bed. I slung my arm around his little shoulders. A long sigh escaped him, and he drifted off to sleep. About to do the same, I gave a habitual pull on the duvet, hauling it up to my ears—the way I liked to sleep—and burrowed into its soft, billowy folds.

Suddenly, as if I had been stuck with a cattle prod, my mind was wide awake, playing a multimedia feed of images: news stories; magazine articles, talking doctor heads, back-to-sleep banners waving in the periphery, warnings of mixing babies and bundling layers of fabric and feathers—very dangerous.

Working to lower my heart rate, I took a few deep breaths. "No, that's not right," I admonished my inner terrorist. "Ted's not a baby anymore. He's fine, see?" I opened my eyes to reassure myself. But only the anti-gravity tuft of hair on the top of Ted's head could be seen above the blankets.

Whipping the duvet down almost to my waist, I rolled onto my back, both actions ensuring I would never fall asleep.

I held out as long as I could, but the urge to roll over and bury myself again became too much to resist.

"Ted," I whispered, hoping to not really waken him, "it's time for you to go back to your own bed." He was half asleep as the two of us padded off to his room. Gratefully,

I slid back between my sheets, and just before I drifted off, I formulated a better plan.

"Dad?"

The room was dark; a thin slice of light fell across the floor. The door was ajar just enough for a little boy to have slipped through.

"Dad?"

Perfect delivery—insistent but *very* quiet.

Pulling the duvet more tightly around my ears blocked out the rest of what we'd rehearsed, and I fell back to sleep.

It wasn't much longer before Marshall outgrew his crib. He spent a few successful weeks sleeping in the little wooden antique bed some friends had loaned us. Or was it only days?

In retrospect, we should have seen the next move coming. Sandwiched between our boys at the head of Ted's double bed, I had just closed the pages of their final bedtime story. Steve was on the floor, propped against the wall. Woody raised himself up at the end of the bed, circled again, and plopped down, pushing his derriere against Marshall's feet.

"How come I always get the butt end?" Marshall asked, peeved.

Something about that struck all of us as terrifically

funny, and we laughed uproariously. Then, with precision timing (and capitalizing on the effervescent mood), Ted delivered his own punch line.

"Can Marshall sleep in my bed tonight?"

We've always said that if you want anything in life, send Ted in to negotiate. Looking back on it, I suspect he'd been looking for a solution to his empty-bed syndrome since the reality-shifting moment he'd acknowledged Lambie was stuffed, but caught off guard by his question, we couldn't come up with a logical reason why not. So from that night till the one when the length of arms and legs meant they no longer fit, our boys shared Ted's bed.

It was the nest from which Steve hatched a wonderful series of nighttime stories, all about two boys named Huck and Ted and their dog named—umm—Woody! It all started on a night when Steve piled in with the guys for their ritual story time.

"Would you like me to *tell* you a story?" I heard him ask as I walked past the open door.

*Lucky them*, I thought, remembering times when I'd been sad and Steve had held me and asked, "Would you like me to tell you a story?" The princess always conquered fear, and love prevailed. It was the ending of every story he told me.

I didn't stay to hear the adventures he conjured up for our boys night after night; I'd have felt like a trespasser on these special moments between a dad and his sons.

I know that the characters Huck and Ted met forces with the likes of Blackbeard. It was just as snow was beginning to swirl in December; the villainous pirate and his nasty buccaneers stole the North Pole with disastrous consequences. It knocked out Santa's navigation system. Christmas was coming, and the workshop overflowed with toys for all the children, but how could Santa make his deliveries flying blind? As the doors on our Advent calendar opened one by one, Huck and Ted were under increasing pressure to put things right or there'd be no presents under the trees!

With that resolved in the nick of time, they temporarily joined Robin Hood and his merry men in Sherwood Forest. I know they recovered Toronto's eighteen hundred foot CN Tower from a gang of international thieves who hoisted it away from the shore of Lake Ontario through the cover of dense fog. Helicopters strong enough to lift it and return it to its original site were well within the realm of the imaginations of Steve and the boys. I know Huck and Ted never had to operate alone, because they always had their trusty dog—umm—

"Woody!" the boys' would shout in unison, filling in the blank. And their friends would be called upon to help out with the story. As situations became more desperate, buddies from school or camp or up the street were recruited to join the forces of good and heroism.

Each night the tale would expand and weave its way through snippets of the life our boys knew—the lake shore we visited or the island at family camp—then it would pick them up and sweep them off to desert lands and ice caps.

"We can change the names to *Marshall* and Ted, you know," Steve told our youngest. Marshall shook his head. He was Huck. He knew that. And he had his brother and their trusty dog. They solved and conquered everything together.

Steve constructed his stories that way on purpose. We weren't advocates of setting up competition between our sons unless it was agreed upon and the rules were clear— like a game of Uno. Then we had fierce fun with competition. But, "Let's see which one of you can be the first to get his coat on" seemed to be just another way of saying, "I'm going to create a situation here, at the end of which *one* of you is going to be a loser." And why would we want that?

If the real goal was to get out the door fast, we'd try to find a reason for them to work together to accomplish it.

So they delighted in Steve's accounts of how a band of two boys and a dog could barricade fortresses against uprising rebels or restart Niagara Falls after water pirates drained the Great Lakes dry. Just when they could hardly bear the suspense of what they were going to do to get out of the fix their adventures had put them in, Steve would pause.

"And *that's* when it happened," Steve would tell them.

"What?!" Ted and Marshall would gasp in anticipation.

"You'll find out tomorrow," Steve said each night, ruffling their hair. After planting a kiss on top of their heads, he tucked Ted and Marshall in for the night. At their feet lay their trusty dog, Woody.

Many years later, in a different house in a different town, Steve and I had just turned in for the night and were reading when the sounds of a new ritual being performed rose from the lower level. We heard and recognized a well-known rhythm; it's from the tune my grandmother called "Shave and a Haircut, Two Bits." Our boys had gone to bed with time to read themselves a story. They slept in separate rooms on the lower level now, but the heads of their respective beds shared a central wall. Being apart from one another certainly hadn't changed their sense of brotherly connection, though. *THUMP, thump, thump, Thump, thump*—that familiar "Shave and a Haircut" cadence shook the wall directly beneath us, in Ted's room.

Steve looked at me, puzzled.

*Thump, thump.*

The muffled response came from the room next door to Ted's—the room where Huck slept.

## 𝒲 Play Outside

Devote a large part of your children's day to physical activity, and have a sizable part of it be outdoors: pulling a toboggan up a snow-covered hill, rolling down a grassy one to climb it again, hiking to find frogs and snakes, carrying a picnic lunch, or digging sandpits in which to bury yourselves at the beach and then jumping in the waves to rinse off the gritty bits. There is method in this madness: physically tired children are ready and happy to go to sleep. If all this sounds too far out of your comfort zone, take the challenge. Set an example and get out there and have fun. *You* might get a better night's sleep, too.

## 𝒲 Bedtime

The first time Ted ever slept through the night, he was twenty-one months old. I woke up around half-past six that morning and bolted from our bed, sure he'd stopped breathing. Amazingly he was still asleep. We had kept Ted on a sleep program, but till then it had seemed to have no effect.

When he was about nine months old, our pediatrician friend even came to stay to help reinforce it, which I interpreted to mean she thought we were cheating (which we weren't). She actually volunteered to get out of bed, go into Ted's room, and tell him, "'Night, 'night, Ted; it's time to go to sleep" at all the clearly specified intervals. "I've never known a child to persist beyond three nights," she assured us on day one. On day four, she said she'd never known a child as determined as Ted. On day five, she went home to sleep.

In retrospect, I realize that he didn't make it through the night as a *baby* because I should have wakened him and nursed him at eleven o'clock, as our doctor had suggested, but by that time of night, I was already in bed, exhausted. Yet even as a *kid*, he still wasn't staying asleep.

So with our firstborn approaching the age of two, and me sitting in the dark weeping as he cried across the hall, I turned to Steve in tears and moaned, "Something has to change. I can't take this anymore." We'd been having talks about having a second child, but as soon as I'd begin to imagine another baby waking in the night, I'd go sleep in the spare room.

Something did change, however: I decided to follow my instincts. Our trusted doctor had advised us against providing bedtime snacks, and since we had followed all his good advice about food and diapers and everything else (except that 11:00 pm infant feeding) and achieved excellent results, we had agreed to follow this rule, too—that is, until that particular night, when I took Ted down to the kitchen after his bath, plopped him in his booster seat, and fed him a little bowl of Cheerios with milk. Then I fed him more Cheerios and a slice of toast with cheese. Then I gave him a banana. It was like filling a bottomless pit. Having finally filled the void, we headed upstairs for toothbrushing and story time. Then 'night, 'night, sleep tight—and he did! Bedtime snacks became my most favorite ritual.

Twelve months later, Ted had a baby brother who, mercifully, turned out to be a very good sleeper.

## Back to the Womb

Ted was born in Australia. The nurses, whom Aussies call "sisters", taught us to bath babies in very deep, wonderfully warm water—a whole tubful of it. I guess it made them feel like going back to the womb, because we watched as our babies floated and lounged and sometimes even fell asleep in the careful hold we were taught to use. So it seemed natural to us that our boys would love their nightly baths.

## Bathtub Toys

There is much for children to learn as they play in water. Allow them a wondrous array of tub toys—not all at once, but rotated frequently to change the mix. Only a few need to be purchased; the rest can be items you already have: a turkey baster, a funnel, margarine tubs, straws, and wine corks from the kitchen cupboards and drawers. Combined with a few of their action figures and plastic boats, these will make for a tubful of fun. Add a plastic tea set and a couple of marbles, and the whole game changes. Get them to predict what will sink and what will float.

If you regularly change the experience, kids will happily anticipate their bathtime. That puts you a step closer to getting them happily to bed, which is the *real* objective. Body soap crayons and bubble bath are fun ways to get clean. Pull the shower curtain shut and create a sprinkle from above as they sit in the bathwater, letting them sail their pirate ships through an imaginary storm on the high seas. Foam shapes designed to stick to the surrounding tiles add a new dimension for storytelling or learning the alphabet. Play some of their favorite music in the background. Give them an unbreakable "mirror" with suction cups on the back to stick to the tub wall, and let them create zany hairstyles secured with lather from tearless shampoo.

## ☙ Bathtime Rules

Keeping rules simple makes them easy to remember and follow. We had four: (1) nobody turns on the faucet, (2) keep the water inside the tub, (3) stay sitting on your bums (for safety's sake), and (4) have fun. Of course, an adult must be on full-time supervision duty. That will be fun for you, too.

As a side note, as you're thinking up rules, try to phrase them in the positive, telling kids what you *want* them to do rather than what you don't want them to do.

## How Kids See Volume and Mass

While still young (at least till seven and perhaps up to eleven), kids don't grasp the concept of conservation of volume. If you pour water from a low flat container into a tall narrow one, a young child tell you that the tall container has more water in it than the flat one did—even though it is exactly the same water they saw poured from one to the other. To them, the higher level means *more*.

You'll see the same stage evident in the kitchen as it pertains to mass. Take a ball of pie pastry or play dough and roll it out flat. Your child will perceive the wide, flat disk as having more dough than the original ball, although it is the same amount of dough with which you started. Eventually, your child will come to understand this concept as the conservation of mass, but it could take a college education before she or he could name the phenomenon. It was the Swiss developmental psychologist Jean Piaget who first noted these developmental stages.

## Fun with Water

Water is a wonderful soother at other times of the day besides bathtime. Outdoors, allow the hose to run in a slow drizzle into a plastic baby bath or kiddie pool. Let your little one fill pails and pots and then empty them into flower beds or the vegetable garden. Or give your child a bucket, some ecofriendly bubbles, and a cloth and let him or her take ride-on trucks and cars through the "car wash." And, of course, there's always the fun of running through the sprinkler.

There are ways and times to combine reasonable water consumption and play while teaching your children to conserve our precious water supply.

Always remember: kids are both waterproof and washable. If it's been raining for days, and you're tired of being housebound, head out in rubber boots or bare feet and delight in the gushes from the eaves trough downspout. Stomp in the puddles. Float sticks down the gutters. Count worms. Squish mud between your toes. Teach your child how to find a rainbow. As the rain is just ending, put the reemerging sun at your back and look straight ahead—if there's a rainbow, that's where it will be.

Indoors, as dinner is being prepared, park your kids in front of the kitchen sink on a chair that is safe for them to stand on—we had a couple of wooden captain's chairs with arms that wrapped around in a semicircle, enclosing our boys against the counter. Put big plastic bibs on them and allow them to puddle around in the sink. Give them measuring spoons, ladles, and odd-ball safe things from a drawer filled with items new to a child—chopsticks, a lemon juicer, a pastry brush, a wire strainer—and let them add a few action figures or plastic animals. Add soap bubbles. They'll get water all over the place (which is easy to wipe up with a bath towel). They may also need a change of clothes—or socks, at least—but you'll have had time to accomplish something nearby in peace, if not quiet.

Until they're old enough to stand at the sink, give them a plastic baby bath on the floor partly filled with dried pasta or beans and allow them to sift, plow, and dig in those. Put a flat sheet or plastic tablecloth from the dollar store underneath to catch the beans that spill. Stay nearby and watchful so your toddlers won't eat the hard legumes—or stuff them up their nostrils.

## 𝒲 Water Safety

Make sure your children learn to swim. The further they go in formal instruction, the safer they will be around water. It is as important as teaching them how to cross a street. And be vigilant.

I came across a family photo recently. At first glance, I smiled at the fun it made me recall. Our family had been given a week's stay at our friends' classic riverfront cottage. Included was the use of a small metal outboard motorboat. In the snapshot, Ted and Marshall, ages six and three, are seated side by side on the middle seat of the boat, and Steve is at the rear, steering. I know those are not nautical terms. I know nothing about boating, which explains why Steve (who had some experience in these things) was driving. The shoreline on either side of the craft was a considerable distance away, and from the size of the wake unfurling behind the boat, it was apparent that we were traveling at a good speed.

And then it struck me. Both boys were dressed in T-shirts and shorts. Period. No personal flotation devices (PFDs)—life jackets, we used to call them.

I was flabbergasted to think that we could possibly have done something so negligent, so irresponsible, as to put our children in a boat without that essential lifesaving piece of apparel. In my mind, I was almost wondering where the hell these boys' mother was, except I already knew. I was the one at the front of the boat, taking the picture. Me—the one who has earned a Bronze Medallion in water safety, who grew up on one of the Great Lakes with a fearful respect for being in or on the water. I missed that step entirely.

We were just lucky nothing happened.

Parents also need to know the dangers of inflatable toys on open bodies of water. If you pop your little one into an inner tube or onto a rubber raft, or any inflated toy, check there is not an offshore breeze. Put your back to the sand and your face to the water; if you feel the breeze on your back, *that's* offshore. That little wind can blow your young child out of your reach in a heartbeat. Within seconds, the child will be in well over his or her head. In a strong breeze, a child will be carried along faster than a capable swimmer can swim. Save inflatable toys for the days with an onshore breeze. But be aware: wind can change direction suddenly.

## Read, Read, Read

Story time follows toothbrushing. Read and read and read to your children. Deliver up poetry and nursery rhymes and fairy tales. From Dennis Lee to Shel Silverstein, plenty of poets will make your kids laugh. And you'll laugh, too. Delight them with age-old fairy tales retold from modern perspectives. Put the books away and *tell* them stories—real or fanciful. Offer them nonfiction from an early stage: books about trucks, puppy breeds, bridges, people, or science. Allow them their favorites and read them again and again. From age-appropriate board books to lift-the-flap books to chapter books, keep reading. And let them read to you, without too much correction. Let them see *you* reading for pleasure, and in the end they will want to read for themselves.

## ❦ Shut Up and Shove Over!

As simplistic as this sounds, Steve and I tried to treat our sons the way adults would expect to be treated. That is, you can't just *hit* them when they do things you don't like (or when they *don't* do things you *would* like). Try walking up behind an adult and whapping him or her across the back of the head; you'll most likely get charged with assault. You can't hit adults, and you must not hit kids.

There were other things we didn't do and things we didn't say. So I got a real shock the summer evening Ted, Marshall, and I were all skooched into Ted's bed for story time. Oh, and Woody was there, too. I was barely through the first few paragraphs of the book they'd chosen for me to read when Ted turned to me, and in the nicest voice said, "Mom, would you please shut up?"

Shut up? *Shut up?!*

I thought Marshall would fall out of bed. Nobody in our house told *anybody* to shut up. I looked at Ted, dumbfounded. What was even odder was that he looked dumbfounded, too.

Before I could finish formulating the thousand questions and mini lectures that had begun swirling in my head, Ted blurted out, "I mean shove over. Could you please shove over?"

I don't know how Sigmund Freud would have

interpreted the slip, but I don't think we ever finished the book that night. It took the three of us a very long time to stop laughing and I couldn't read through the tears, anyway. Even when I tried to pick the story back up, one of us would dissolve into hysterics and the story line would be lost once again.

## ☙ Learning to Wait

The Huck and Ted series of stories helped our boys learn about delayed gratification—a sort of save-the-best-for-last approach. That's not easy for little ones, who want what they want immediately. This also applies to many adults. Steve feared Ted and Marshall would mutiny at his withholding of a story's outcome, so sometimes he would give them just a tidbit from the next night's installment. That's all he *could* give them, since *he* didn't have a clue how things were going to turn out, either!

## ☙ Tuck-In Service

When our sons reached the age of about seven or eight it no longer seemed appropriate for me, their mother, and then Steve, their father, to see them naked. They would bathe themselves, brush their teeth, get into their pajamas, and call out for "tuck-in service."

That meant story time and a hug and a kiss goodnight. "Tuck-in service" got shortened to TIS—a call we would hear from upstairs when our attention was desired. One night, when Marshall had been invited to a friend's for a sleepover, Steve and I laughed when we heard Ted yell, "TIT!" Tuck in Ted is what he meant, but we had to point out to him how some acronyms just don't work in polite company.

# CHAPTER 5

## *Drop By Any Time for Beer and Wine*

"I DON'T EAT ORANGE FOOD."

I looked at the bowl of cream of tomato soup and the plate of grilled cheese sandwiches with carrot sticks on the side. "Really?" I asked, slightly stunned by this lunch hour revelation, "Since when?"

"Since my other mother told me I don't have to," Marshall announced.

"Oh." I drew a breath as I counted to ten by fives. "Well, until that nice other mother comes to make lunch for you, this is what we're having."

Frankly, the woman was starting to get on my nerves. Everything was "my other mother *this*" and "my other mother *that*." She never made Marshall wash his hands before meals or finish his peas or wear what was set out on his bed. In fact, according to Marshall, his entire other family was nicer than ours, taking him places we wouldn't or couldn't afford and buying him everything he wanted. At that family's house, the world was Marshall's oyster.

It didn't seem fair. I was left with all the discipline issues. And there were some. Like the clothing wars. The small skirmishes I tried to concede easily: cutting every tag from tops and bottoms because they caused itching; waiting patiently for shoes to be tested before purchase to determine whether there was room inside for Marshall to cross his toes easily. Other battles, though, drew more opposition, on both our parts.

Admittedly, Marshall, by nature, was resistant to change. It would take mid-June sweltering heat and withering humidity to convince him to peel out of his winter wardrobe and make the adjustment to a cooler selection of clothes. Conversely, as fall days grew chillier, he'd refuse to give up what he'd grown accustomed to wearing all summer. One particularly crisp October morning, over breakfast, I pointed out to him that this was a preschool morning and his group would be starting the day outdoors on the play equipment. "And because it's so cold out, you'll need to wear long pants and a long-sleeved shirt," I explained. Everyone else had made the switch weeks before.

"No-o-o," he resisted, as he slid off his chair. "I'm going to wear a T-shirt and T-pants."

*Makes sense*, I thought, smiling to myself as I followed him out of the kitchen. If we call a shirt with short sleeves a T-shirt, why wouldn't we call trousers that end at the knee T-pants?

"Actually," I called after him as he reached the stairs, "I

set out some pants for you to choose from. Let me know which ones you want to wear."

Anxious to observe the process, I caught up with him as he rounded the corner into his bedroom. Laid out in a colorful array were a pair of blue jeans, a pair of black jeans, a pair of black jeans with leather cowboy fringe down the sides, wide-wale green corduroys, and an identical pair of corduroys in bright orange.

Marshall stopped, took one sweeping look at the selection, and said, "I don't wear pants that have pockets"—picking, in a nanosecond, the one variable that would eliminate all my offerings. It's not what his *other* mother would have said, but having been so deftly, so *easily*, outwitted by a child, I snapped. "They *make* pants without pockets," I told him. "They're called *tights*, and girls wear them."

That was not one of my finest mommy moments. When pushed to the edge, I reached for the finely honed weapon of sarcasm. *How is that other mother always so nice?"* I wondered. Maybe she had a spa membership. Or a therapist. Or a nanny.

I thought I had met her one day outside the grocery store.

"Excuse me," I heard from over my left shoulder, and I turned to see her standing directly behind me. It turned out it wasn't her, but I was sure this was what Marshall's other mother looked like. She was a slim, polished woman, in perfect makeup, dressed in perfect layers of early spring black. Or was it late winter black? It didn't matter; no matter how many layers she put on, she'd still look slim. Her sun-streaked hair was pulled up and back in a tousle that showed off her diamond stud earrings. She also wore a look of genuine concern. Actually, it was more like alarm, but it didn't seem to detract from her natural elegance. "Is everything all right?"

My chin dropped to my chest in defeat as I visualized the scenario from her perspective.

My driver's door stood open, the way I'd left it, blocking access to the parking spot beside mine. The backseat passenger door was also open, and the child's booster seat inside was empty. Bags of groceries were piled in mounds on the seats and the floor. I was crouched on the asphalt outside the back passenger door, so my back was to her, but I knew she was looking over the shoulder of my dusty barn coat at Marshall. He was standing stock-still in front of me, defiantly encased as I held his upper arms.

"Is everything all right?" she asked again.

"No, obviously everything is not all right," I admitted, trying my hardest to sound like a nice lady. "I appreciate your concern, and it's very good of you to stop and ask, but I can't drive home because my son keeps undoing his seat belt as soon as I start the car. I have been back here a thousand times to explain that we can't leave until he agrees to stay buckled up, but he refuses to cooperate, so we're just going to stand here in the parking lot while we wait for him to get things back on track."

"But he's in bare feet," she observed.

"I know that," I told her, spying his boots on the floor inside the van.

"And he's standing in snow."

The breath whooshed out of me. "I know that, too," I said in complete defeat, looking at the patch of late March slush under Marshall's small feet.

That's how the whole thing had started, really. It had been the clothing war of the day: up and down the aisles of the grocery store, Marshall had kicked off his boots and pulled off his socks until I'd just given up. I'd managed to get them on him again as we exited the store, but by the time we reached our van, he'd reached down and yanked everything off till he was down to his little piggies.

And then he'd started with the seat belt.

"I just think he must be cold." She was clearly sympathetic to him.

"Yes, I suspect he is." I agreed. "What I'm hoping is that when he gets cold *enough*, he'll get back into his seat belt, put on his boots, and we can go home. Unless you have a better idea."

She was nice enough about it. I know she didn't want to walk away, but she did. I think something about her courage to confront what she saw shifted things. Maybe Marshall was embarrassed or finally just cold enough, because right away he climbed back into the van, left his seat belt alone after I buckled it, and we drove home.

Although footwear wasn't the only item to create issues, it caused its fair share of problems. Like the struggle we had over a new pair of shoes. Marshall picked them: red runners with white rubber soles and fat white laces. He loved them. In the driveway, at home, the day before starting back to school from the summer holidays, he demonstrated the best of their features: fast starts, great braking, terrific turning ratio. They were super shoes. Until—

"Red shoes? You're wearing *red* shoes?" a kindergarten classmate with a critical eye for junior fashion scoffed, and Marshall's new sneakers disappeared into the back of his closet. It took me weeks to figure out what had happened.

"Marshall," I pushed, "it's no one else's business what you wear on your feet, and you don't need to worry about what other people think about your shoes, anyway. You loved them, we paid for them, so wear them." But he wouldn't. And he didn't. Besides, he told us, his *other* family wouldn't make him.

It didn't matter that there *was* no other family—they existed only as figments of Marshall's imagination—they were starting to tick me off. "Tell you what," I suggested one day, "how would you like to invite your other family over for a visit? Dad and I would be very interested to meet them." What with them being such nice folks, and all. "We could have dinner together. You could choose the menu."

Days passed. I asked how the invitation was progressing.

"Oh, they're coming," Marshall informed me. "You should serve them wine and beer. I'll let you know when."

Weeks passed, so I asked for an update.

"They can't come," Marshall informed me, matter-of-factly.

"I'm very sorry to hear that," I said. "I was really looking forward to meeting them. Perhaps they can come another time."

"No." Marshall seemed certain.

"Why not?" I asked. "Do you know what happened?"

"Yup," he nodded solemnly. "They died."

I was stunned. "*Died*?" I repeated. "How?"

"In a fire."

And that was the end of those very nice people—which meant, I supposed happily, that Marshall was coming to live with us full-time.

Many years later, as we were all dressing for a special function, Marshall emerged from his room wearing his navy blazer, a buttoned shirt tucked into gray flannel pants, a black belt, and—scruffy brown skateboarding shoes the size of river barges.

"Marshall," I intercepted him on his way downstairs. "Where are the black loafers we bought you to wear today?"

"I don't like them," he told me. "These will be fine."

Having vowed to be nicer, having vowed to not take him outside and stand him barefoot in the snow again, I firmly but politely disagreed; "Those shoes don't go with the outfit, and for the occasion, they're not appropriate. This is a special day. It is socially acceptable to dress accordingly. People would expect it."

For one brief moment, I thought that nice lady from his incinerated family was going to rise from the ashes, but I was wrong. Instead, Marshall unearthed a carbon-dated nugget I had long forgotten.

"I thought you said I don't have to worry about what people think of my shoes."

## ❦ Time-Out

After recounting stories to friends who are wiser than I am, I learned a couple of things: it is possible to give your child too many options, and when kids get cold enough, they will put on long pants.

I also learned that Steve and I had the time-out thing backward. Our deal was this: if you misbehaved after two warnings, you had to go to your room, and you couldn't come out until the whole thing had been thought through and you were ready to make amends.

Unfortunately, that gave all the power to the disciplined child—he could come out instantly or wait forty-five minutes and have a nap in the meantime. That essentially put us, as parents, in time out while we waited to get on with errands or schedules.

Generally, Marshall used his time-outs as opportunities to tear his bedroom apart. By the time he said he was ready to cooperate, the entire contents of his dresser drawers and bookcase would be strewn across the floor and his bed would be stripped of its linens. That meant we had to send him back in to clean up the mess, which he was disinclined to do, thank you very much, which meant we had to put him back in his room till he was ready to. You get the picture.

There was one day, though, when Steve and I thought we had finally won the battle. I had followed

Steve as he carried Marshall upstairs, put him in his room, and told him, through the closed door, "You can come out when you're ready to cooperate."

The two of us were just walking away, barely steps from Marshall's room, when we heard, from inside, "I *am* ready to cooperate."

Steve and I stared at each other. Never had we thought we'd see the time when our strong-willed younger child would be so quick to comply. We were just in the process of exchanging self-satisfied, congratulatory grins when Marshall *finished* his incomplete sentence: " . . . you idiots!"

Steve and I had to race to our master bathroom and shut ourselves in so that Marshall couldn't hear our reaction. With our faces buried in thick bath towels and with my legs crossed to keep from wetting my pants, we both laughed until we cried.

So eat your Wheaties to keep your strength up, and remember to keep a sense of humor. There will be days like this for you, too.

## ⚥ Safety Tip

When you're in a parking lot, teach your kids to watch for a car's illuminated clear white taillights that indicate the driver has put the vehicle in reverse. Kids don't know what those lights mean, so explain the danger and model for them not stepping behind a car that is backing up.

## ⚥ Options

There were times when an invitation or opportunity arose to do something on an outing that might have required a change of clothes or a piece of sports equipment. Occasionally, the boys might say *with conviction* that no, they weren't going to swim or play ball or whatever with those people in that place.

Our simple response was to insist the boys take their swimsuits or baseball gloves or whatever, saying, "If you take it with you, you have a choice." It didn't mean they had to join in, but without their suits or ball gloves or whatever, they would give up the option of changing their minds. Our sons use the approach to this day.

## ⚥ Adult Tantrums

Many times, Steve gently reminded me that it is not our job, as parents, to make our sons cooperate. It is our job to help them grow.

He also had the wisdom to let me know when I'd reached the limit on lecturing our sons. My scoldings had the potential to brew into full-blown tirades. "They got the message," Steve would say, touching me lightly on the shoulder, "so that's enough."

"No, it's *not*," I might hiss in return; there was much more I could add. The longer I talked, the deeper into my vocabulary I could delve for descriptors of my indignation. "I'm not *done*!"

Turning me gently, but now firmly, by the shoulder, Steve would look at me coolly and calmly and simply insist, "Yes, you are."

That was a good thing for me as I learned to parent. It took a very wise, and most likely brave, friend to really get the point across to me, though. Responding to a child's tantrum with a tantrum of my own was simply counterproductive. As I reflect on that wisdom, it reminds me of a long-ago campaign by the United Church of Canada against the death penalty. They distributed buttons that read: WHY KILL SOMEONE WHO KILLED SOMEONE TO PROVE THAT KILLING SOMEONE IS WRONG?

## ❦ Setting Limits

Experts tell us that it constitutes neglect not to give our children boundaries. Discipline frees a child to play, to learn, and to grow within safe, reasonable, and consistent boundaries. Only when children learn that the *rules* aren't going to change can they begin to understand that it is their *behavior* that must be modified. Once they know where the limits lie, they are free to play and explore within them without fear of negative consequences.

Consistency in your rules takes a lot of planning, discussion, and agreement with your parenting partner. Without it, however, your child is forever at risk of breaking the rules, because the rules are ever changing and therefore impossible to predict. Your children will test those limits over and over again. They're just checking to see whether the rules are still the same as they were yesterday—or five minutes ago.

## 🌷Respect

Some parents feel uncomfortable saying no (and meaning it) to their children's requests for material things and/or privileges, for fear their kids won't *like* them.

I believe that in the course of their lifetimes, Ted and Marshall will have the chance to make and keep many, *many* friends, but they have only one mom and one dad. They don't need us as friends—nor do I think they *want* us as friends. We are their parents— a privileged relationship. It is our job to act as parents, providing safety and loving guidance on our sons' paths to adulthood.

So if you have to choose between being liked and

being respected, go for being respected every time. Your children will end up liking you for it.

Having said that, I do not believe that children are duty-bound to respect their parents; some parents say and do things that render them unworthy of a child's respect. I believe that we, as parents, are duty-bound to be *worthy* of our children's respect. We do this by modeling the ethics, the character, and the standards of behavior we are trying to foster. We speak respectfully to our children. We respect their privacy. We respect their individuality, and at all times we respect their humanity. Only then might we expect them to treat us the same way in return.

## Strict but Fair

"Do you know you have a reputation?"

As a teacher, one of my responsibilities was to patrol the schoolyard. This September day a young girl walked alongside me as I kept my eye on other students. She was new to my Grade Five class. And she was watching my face for a reaction.

"No," I told her. Then I stopped talking, hoping she would continue.

"Yeah," she nodded. "Kids who know you say you're strict but fair."

I was good with that as a teacher, and I'm good with that as a mom.

## ▼ Hairstyle Choices

There are times when something matters far more to one parent than it does to the other. Rather than showing our sons a divided front, Steve and I chose to let the parent who was more invested handle the matter or simply have his or her way.

For instance, I never wanted to have arguments with our children about their hair. I had cried far too many tears, as a girl, over how my parents forced me to wear mine. You would only have to see my school pictures to understand. So Steve agreed to the approach of allowing our sons complete control over their haircuts and hairstyles.

Then, in Grade One, Marshall caught on to a popular fad and started growing a rattail—one long curling tendril of hair that slithered down the nape of his neck from an otherwise short haircut. Neither Steve nor I liked the look, especially the way some people grew them halfway down their backs, so, to Marshall's credit, when we explained how uncomfortable we felt about it, he agreed to keep his short. Next we tried a humorous approach, explaining to him about the rattail fairy that came in the night with scissors and left five bucks on your pillow in exchange for the unflattering tendril of hair. Marshall just laughed. So we waited it out, until one day he told our stylist to cut it off.

Years later, Ted decided on dreadlocks. Although they appeared to be the result of years of neglect, they actually required a fair amount of maintenance that involved a pot of beeswax and a back-combing motion. Again, Steve and I encouraged this display of confidence, this flirtation with fashion, even though we didn't particularly like the look. What was most important was that our son felt good about himself.

We were surprised the day Ted returned to the stylist to have his dreads shorn off. "Why?" we asked him. His answer was simple: they smelled.

## ❦ Outsmarting a Fad

Before you automatically blurt no to every request your child makes, consider coming at an issue from a different, more positive—possibly more *creative*—angle.

One of my biggest fears as Ted and Marshall approached their teenage years was that they might opt for permanent reminders of temporary fads. I know I'm not alone in this; I read about a mom who had a great approach handling her teenage daughter's request for a tattoo. The mom told the girl that yes, she *could* get a tattoo. There was only one condition: the girl had to decide on one design and spend an entire year committed to simply *wanting* that particular piece of artwork emblazoned on her body—without changing her mind. If she could do that—be committed to one image for a full twelve months—then at the end of the year, she could actually get it.

The girl started off convinced that at the end of the designated period, she would have Betty Boop inked onto her upper arm. That lasted a while. Then it was Tweety Bird. At the age of twenty-six, that daughter still had no tattoos.

I had a different approach, which apparently worked; I've been assured, at our sons' current ages of twenty-five and twenty-two, that neither of them has pierced or inked anything. I simply told Ted and Marshall that if they were thinking about getting any tattoos or body piercings, it was fine with me—as long as they understood *I* would be doing them.

# CHAPTER 6

## *I'll Show You Idiot-Proof*

I DON'T REALLY *LIKE* BAKING. I DON'T THINK MY MOTHER DID either, given some of the desserts she used to serve when I was a kid. Prune Whip. I don't think there ever was a recipe for that (not that you'd want it, anyway) but essentially it involved whipped cream and whipped prunes. I did like the frozen logs she created with alternating layers of chocolate wafers and vanilla ice cream. She frosted them with whipped cream and sprinkled a grating of semisweet chocolate over the top. They were tasty.

But you'll notice these dishes required a refrigerator, not an oven. Mind you, there were also the drained canned peaches she used to line up smartly in a baking pan. When they were put under the broiler, the marshmallow she popped inside each little round cavity would puff up and get toasty, gooey brown. They were hard to eat, though, skittering away in the bowl the way they did on their wet, round bottoms. And I don't think we could really consider that baking.

In all fairness to my mother, I know she made other desserts, but these are the ones that made a lasting impression on me. I grew up preferring salt. More than likely, that was on account of my mom, too. She put salt on anything: steak, apples, cantaloupe, watermelon, garden tomatoes eaten whole, right out of your hand. To this day, I can pass up a rocky road, triple-fudge, double-scoop waffle cone, no sweat, but if anyone starts selling biscuity herbed cones mounded with scoops of creamy hot garlic mashed potatoes, topped with a pat of sweet butter, a pinch of sea salt, and a grinding of black pepper, I'm doomed.

Besides, baking's fussy. Cooking is much more forgiving. Lasagna that calls for a tablespoon of basil or parsley will easily tolerate you heaping or skimping on the quantity. Try that with baking powder—or, for that matter, baking soda.

As an enrichment activity to enhance part of the Grade Five curriculum, I once had my class bake carrot cake. Small groups were responsible for different parts of the recipe: sifting flour, peeling carrots, measuring the ingredients, and stirring the batter. When it was all put together—numerous pans of it—we delivered the oblong glass dishes to the home of one of the students whose mom had kindly volunteered to oversee the baking, seeing as how the oven in the staff room wasn't so reliable.

Imagine my embarrassment when she called forty

minutes later to report that the batter was overflowing the pans and spewing never-ending waves of shredded carrot, muck, and cinnamon-scented bubbles over the bottom element and into the base of her stove.

It was at that point in our conversation I heard her smoke detector go off.

Lesson learned? Be sure your kids know the difference between these two measurement abbreviations: tbsp. and tsp. Sorry, Mrs. Hahn.

I couldn't just let the project end that way, of course. My students were all primed to try the dessert they'd worked together to create, even if it did involve vegetables, and, besides, the icing was already made. So that night, in my home, I started from scratch and baked up another whole batch of carrot cakes.

Many years later and in a different kitchen, Ted arrived home from his Grade One class for lunch.

"Mom," he asked, "what's the difference between a pie and a cake?"

Instantly, my skin began to prickle with that familiar yet uncomfortable "not-a-good-enough-mom" reaction. Like a rash.

"Ted," I chided him, "you know what a cake is. You get one every year on your birthday, right?"

"Yeah," he said, nodding. Then, after a moment, he cocked his head and asked, "But then, what's a pie?"

Hmm. Reflecting on the menus I'd been serving for the past number of months—okay, years—I silently acknowledged it was probably time to stop serving only fresh fruit for dessert.

We could certainly *buy* a pie, but it was unlikely we would ever make one, since pastry involved small quantities of cold water and a large amount of flour. That's the precise recipe I used to make paste when I was a kid.

Paste, or mucilage (that's what they used to call it—mucilage) was a clear brown liquid that came in a bell-shaped jar. The jar had a red rubber nib with a slash in it for dabbing the mucilage on whatever you needed to get stuck. If we ran out of mucilage, we would mix flour and water in a bowl and use that instead. It would stick *anything* to anything else.

So pastry, which seemed to me straddled a narrow gap between baking and paste-making, was definitely out. But we had out-of-town friends coming for the weekend, and, in a moment of pure amnesia, I decided that the boys and I could make carrot cake to have when our guests arrived on Friday night. With any luck, there would be lots left over, and I wouldn't have to make something else to serve for dessert Saturday night. Bonus!

So Ted, Marshall, and I spent Friday afternoon grating and measuring and sifting—being ever so careful about the tbsps. and the tsps.— and greasing the pan. Woody helped by licking up all the carrot bits from the floor.

When the timer beeped, indicating the cake was finished, I pulled the pan from the oven and, with a grand flourish, showed Ted and Marshall what we'd created.

"Isn't it supposed to be flat on top?" Ted asked. Assessing the dip in the center of our cake, I assured the boys that if we just filled the hollow space in the center with lots of icing, our dessert would look surprisingly expert. We set the pan out to cool and headed to the video store for some kids' movies.

I was first through the door when we arrived home from our errand. When I think about it now, I recall that Woody was sitting pretty quietly in the hallway, and, when I *really* think about it, I can recollect his canine version of the look we all know means "Don't go in the kitchen." But I was in the middle of explaining to Marshall what the word *macho* meant (from the song "Macho, Macho Man" that had been playing on the car radio), so I was caught completely off guard to see the cake pan sitting on the floor in front of the stove. The space in the pan had been neatly divided in two, lengthwise. One half had cake in it. The other half didn't.

Ted and Marshall must have thought their mother had palsy or had suffered a stroke, since they couldn't see around the corner of the kitchen island to see what I had seen. I just groaned, midsentence, and fell to my knees.

Of course, just like back in my teaching days, it meant having to start all over with the carrot cake recipe; our guests were already on their way, I had nothing else for dessert, and, besides, the icing was already made.

That calamity was not entirely my fault, but there have been a few others—well, a number of others—that I admit to. Like the banana chocolate-chip oatmeal muffins. With the pan nicely in the oven and the dishes cleaned up, it was time for a little break. I opened the microwave to reheat my coffee, and there, in the Pyrex measuring cup, sat the melted butter that was supposed to be part of the batter. A fairly essential part, it turns out. I tried (optimistically) just slathering butter onto the muffins once they had finished baking, but that just gave them the texture of greased hay and the density of a hockey puck.

Then there were the fifty-six Christmas shortbread cookies I made using unsalted butter by mistake. We all waited patiently as pan after pan of pale, warm, uniformly round and flat cookies cooled on wire racks on the counters. Each was beautifully decorated with its own tiny silver candy ball. They had the right texture, for sure. But they tasted like flour and cornstarch.

By the time Marshall could see countertops, he would assess what had been laid out there. Anytime he spotted eggs, flour, sugar, and butter—even within distant proximity to one another—he'd moan, "Oh no, Mom's baking!" My reputation spread beyond just our kitchen. When a relative found out I'd taken to ordering our boys' birthday cakes from the local grocery store, she sent me a recipe copied from her files. Across the top, in handwriting, she had renamed it for me: Idiot-Proof Chocolate Cake.

I read a lot of recipes. I'm good at predicting a great-tasting appetizer, soup, or main course, but sometimes I get sidetracked (or delusional) and find myself poring over directions for magnificent desserts. The list of ingredients and instructions for Idiot-Proof Chocolate Cake were very straightforward, but it did involve wet ingredients and dry ingredients, so I knew there was the potential for mishap, if not outright disaster. I'm happy to say it turned out to be reliable. Everything goes into one bowl. Then it all gets poured into a Bundt pan. Even so, there were a few mistakes I could (and did) make: forgetting to add the chocolate chips to the batter and neglecting to grease the pan being two things of lesser consequence. Then there was the day I had taken Ted and Marshall into the back yard to play. I discovered that our smoke detector is a much more insistent reminder to take a cake out of the oven than the quiet little beeping of our stove timer.

Imagine my delight, then, when one autumn day I came upon a recipe in a parenting magazine for something I *knew* I could make without fail. With Ted and Marshall positioned on their captains' chairs at the kitchen island, their sleeves rolled high and their hopes even higher, we mixed ingredients and rolled and patted. Using seasonal cookie cutters, we cut out pumpkins and ghosts and bats. We poked small holes through their tops, then baked them all to perfection. Our plan was to paint them with orange, black, and white tempera paint, hang them from threads, and make Halloween mobiles.

Eat them? Not on your life! My new favorite recipe was for salt dough—never intended for human consumption.

## ❦ In the Kitchen

The boys and I spent a lot of time in the kitchen. It clearly wasn't all for baking, but some of it was. I've always figured kids come to us waterproof and fully washable, so letting them get messy has never been an issue for me. We had three simple rules for cooking: wash your hands before you start; no finger licking, and have fun.

It wasn't always something edible we were working to create. On a rainy day, we'd spread out sheets of finger-painting paper and make goopy prints and patterns using chocolate pudding. On a sunny day, we'd take the activity outside and, dressed in old bathing suits, use the pudding as body paint. A run through the sprinkler or an encounter with Woody would clean up most of the mess.

In May, we hunted the woods for wild leeks and fiddlehead ferns and served them up with spring suppers. Each June, we would make strawberry freezer jam that required no cooking. We tried the low-sugar variety, but we didn't really like it, so we went back to the recipe that uses far more sugar than fruit. Most of the jars we gave away as end-of-year gifts to teachers and such. We didn't eat much ourselves, but it was a fun field-to-finish project, from picking berries at the farm to capping each jar.

Every Thanksgiving, we made turkey cookies from a

simple sugar cookie recipe I found in an old cookbook. After cutting the rolled dough into turkey shapes, we "painted" the heads and tails with a red-food-coloring egg wash and decorated them with sprinkles before baking.

At Christmas we put together gingerbread houses. The first year, we made the gingerbread from scratch, but much preferring the category of *crafts* to the category of *baking*, I thereafter resorted to buying the kit from the grocery store. The easiest way to stick the walls together is to dip their edges into melted brown sugar. Just a nonstick frying pan and lots of brown sugar will do the trick. This isn't something you let your kids do. The sugar gets as hot as molten lead and stays that hot on your skin for quite a while, so don't touch it, and don't let it touch *you*. Be warned, too, that if you leave the pan on the burner too long, the whole mess starts to smolder. But if you keep the temperature just right, the sugar turns the consistency of lava and quickly dries like concrete.

Once the houses were assembled, Ted and Marshall would take over the fun of icing and sticking candies to everything. Mini ice cream cones, painted green with food coloring and water, then turned upside down, became little Christmas trees for the yard. Tubes of tinted icing from the baking aisle at the supermarket provided the material for adding swags of colored lights and such to the tiny trees and the eaves of the small cottages or a wreath to the door.

As the boys' abilities and imaginations expanded, so did the shopping list for their landscape designs. Dry cereal and every form of snack food from the bulk bins were transformed into woodpiles, fence posts, walkways, and patios. Miniature elves, snowmen, Santa, and sleighs were scrounged from the box of tree ornaments to complete the streetscape. Everything was stuck to something else with some form of sugar. After New Year's Day, the boys were given the chance to eat their creations. They never consumed much—after all, it was food that should have been dusted before serving.

## Candy and Pizza

Our sons never developed much of a sweet tooth. They were allowed access to their Halloween loot with few restrictions. On days they stayed at school for lunch, they had permission to choose two items out of the collection to put in their lunch pails. A dental hygienist will tell you to encourage your kids to eat the candy before everything else in the lunch pail (which must make dental hygienists very popular with children). Finishing off their meal with something like celery or carrot sticks, instead of toffee, helps clean the sugar off their teeth, reducing the chance of decay.

At some point, maybe late in November, Ted and Marshall would agree to throw out the remaining stash of junk—since it had reached the point of requiring dusting.

Although neither son was big on sweets, both of them really liked pizza. I found an easy recipe for the dough, and every now and then, on a weekend night, the boys and I would work together to make up a batch—yeast and all—so everybody could create a pizza to his or her own liking. The hard part was getting the dough stretched out to form a nice round base that wasn't full of holes. So one day after school, we drove to a nearby pizzeria and got a helpful demonstration from the very nice man in the kitchen.

# RECIPES

## Idiot-Proof Chocolate Cake

1 box devil's food cake mix
1-4-ounce package instant chocolate pudding
1 cup sour cream
1/2 cup canola oil, plus extra for greasing pan
1/2 cup water
4 eggs
1 cup chocolate chips

1 tub chocolate icing

decorative sprinkles

Preheat oven to 350°F.

Combine cake mix, pudding, sour cream, canola oil, water, and eggs. Beat with an electric mixer on medium speed for 4 minutes. Stir in chocolate chips. Pour batter into a 12-cup Bundt pan greased with canola oil.

Bake 50–60 minutes until a toothpick inserted in the center comes out clean. Cool, then turn cake out onto a cake plate.

Frost with chocolate icing. Top with decorative sprinkles.

## Carrot Cake

CAKE

2 cups white sugar

1-1/2 cups canola oil, plus extra for greasing pan

4 eggs

2 cups flour

2 teaspoons baking powder

2 teaspoons baking soda

2 teaspoons cinnamon

1 teaspoon salt

3 cups grated carrots

1 cup chopped pecans

ICING

1-4-ounce package Philadelphia cream cheese, softened

1/2 stick butter, softened

1/2 cup confectioner's sugar

1 teaspoon pure vanilla extract

Preheat oven to 350°F.

Blend sugar and oil in a large mixing bowl. Add eggs one at a time, beating as each is added. Mix well.

In a separate bowl, mix flour, baking powder, baking soda, cinnamon, and salt.

Add the dry ingredients gradually to the wet mixture. Add carrots and pecans last. Mix lightly, and pour batter into a lightly oiled 9 x 13 inch baking pan. Bake 45 minutes. Let cool at a height your dog can't reach.

Combine cream cheese, butter, confectioner's sugar, and vanilla extract. Beat with an electric mixer until creamy.

When cake is completely cool, frost with icing.

## Lasagna

MEAT MIXTURE

1 pound extra-lean ground beef

1 clove garlic, minced

1 tablespoon dried parsley flakes

1 tablespoon dried basil

1-1/2 teaspoons salt

2 cups diced canned tomatoes

2-6-ounce cans tomato paste

1-10-ounce package dried lasagna noodles

COTTAGE CHEESE MIXTURE

3 cups creamed cottage cheese

2 eggs, beaten

2 teaspoons salt

1/2 teaspoon black pepper

2 tablespoons dried parsley flakes

1/2 cup grated Parmesan cheese

1 pound mozzarella cheese, grated

Preheat oven to 375°F.

Brown meat and spoon off fat. Add garlic, parsley, basil, salt, tomatoes, and tomato paste. Simmer uncovered 30 minutes. Stir occasionally.

Cook noodles according to package directions. Rinse and drain.

Combine cottage cheese, eggs, salt, pepper, parsley, and Parmesan cheese.

Line bottom of a 9 x 13 inch baking pan with a single layer of noodles. Spread with half of cottage cheese mixture. Sprinkle almost half of the grated mozzarella on top. Spread half of the meat mixture over all. Repeat the layers in order: a single layer of noodles, the remaining cottage cheese mixture, nearly half of the mozzarella, and the remaining meat mixture.

Bake for 30 minutes. Sprinkle the remaining mozzarella over the top and let stand 10–15 minutes before serving.

## ❦ Parents and Perfection

I would never have set out to intentionally waste all the ingredients I have thrown into the garbage over time, but I think there is great value in what Ted and Marshall and I learned from my repeated kitchen failures.

Not everything turns out the way you hope or plan. It's okay to make mistakes. It's okay to keep trying. It's okay to give up. Failure served with a huge dollop of humor is much easier to swallow.

And, most important, moms and dads are not perfect. We all know people (or we *are* those people) who, through their adult years, cling to the notion that the way they were raised was the *right* way. But that assumes that our parents knew exactly what they were doing and made flawless decisions. That just can't be.

Trying to duplicate the life our parents created simply chains us to the past (making the same mistakes over again) and robs us of the chance to grow.

As a young teacher, I was given the life-enhancing opportunity to live with a friend's family for a year. At first I had a hard time focusing on the lively conversations that took place over and after dinner because I kept getting distracted by the different way they did things.

I'd been taught as a girl that "our way" was the "proper way," and that had to mean that these nice people weren't polite. But that didn't seem right. So I stopped paying attention to what anybody was doing with his or her elbows and forks and realized that when I was growing up, I had missed out on the experience of good-humored fun at mealtime.

My parents were right to teach good manners to their children. I just decided that when I became a parent, I would tweak their model by throwing a few grapes.

# CHAPTER 7

## *A Night at the Primrose Motel*

"DAD?" MARSHALL'S ANXIOUS WHISPER FROM THE BACKSEAT pierced the tension. "Can you see?"

The snowstorm had steadily increased in ferocity over the past half hour. As we edged our way out of the little town, drifts began blowing across the highway. Millions of tiny oncoming flakes, illuminated by our headlights, created a hypnotic, disorienting tunnel against the black sky. Like that hyper-speed scene from the *Star Wars* movie, but life-threatening.

"No." The air whooshed out of Steve as he admitted, "No, Marsh, I can't."

We did a U-turn in the municipal yard at the edge of the town we'd just passed through. The cars that had been following Steve's taillights did the same. Retracing our path, we stopped at the convenience store we'd noticed farther back. Steve bought the last three toothbrushes, a tube of toothpaste, four submarine sandwiches, and some drinks. I called the only motel listed in the yellow pages of the phone directory. It was the sole place of lodging within forty minutes in any given direction.

"Primrose Motel," a female voice answered.

I asked for two double rooms.

"We only have one room left," the woman informed me. "It has two twin beds."

"But there are four of us," I explained. "Do you have any cots?"

They did, but she wasn't sure they'd fit.

"Please try," I begged.

Steve drove through the swirling snow, following the directions we'd been given, back out into the countryside. When we finally pulled off the highway into the motel parking lot, we were tense and tired but relieved to get off the road. We checked in at the office, turned the key in the lock of unit 12, and pushed the door.

Clang! It hit solid resistance and stopped, open only a wedge. We peered into the space. Four small beds filled the entire room. There were wall-to-wall mattresses on narrow metal frames. So we pulled off our boots, stepped through the small opening, and climbed up onto the first of the cots.

Of course, the boys thought it was funny; the only space at ground level was in the bathroom. Fortunately the door to it opened inward, so at least there was some privacy. Not that we'd be getting undressed or changed into something different. We'd made the trip to the city for a matinee performance of Handel's *Messiah*—a pre-

Christmas hit of culture. Thus, we were all dressed up and had nothing else to wear. As we all peeled off the most formal and restrictive pieces of our attire—blazers, ties, belts, pantyhose—and took turns washing up, I searched the room for a phone book. Not finding one, I used directory assistance and placed a call to let the dog sitter know Woody would be having another sleepover, thank you.

That done, we flopped down on our respective beds. Ted grabbed the remote and started flipping through channels on the small-screen TV. Only one station came in loud and clear.

Julie Andrews was just cresting the mountaintop—twirling, arms held wide, singing. Steve joined in, belting out the words. Louder than Julie.

The hills were alive with the sound of—

"Mucus." Steve crooned his improvisation.

My head snapped sideways. "What?" I demanded. "What did you just say?"

"That's what all my friends called this movie," he explained. *The Sound of Mucus.*

Ted and Marshall got the joke the first time and were snorting chocolate milk out their noses. So much for the day's attempts at refinement.

Music had been an integral part of our family life right from the time Ted and Marshall could spontaneously create a marching band of two from the variety of instruments we had in the house: whistles, toy drums, tin flutes, harmonicas, cymbals, plastic ukuleles, tambourines, and maracas.

In fact, at the first hint the band had started up, Woody would jump up from his resting place. *Thump, thump, thump;* we'd hear him climb the stairs. *Boom!* He'd butt the linen closet door open with the flat top of his head. *Crash!* Using his paw, he'd tip the plastic bin we stored there, scattering pint-size instruments across the floor.

*Jingle, jingle. Thump, thump, thump, thump.* Having sorted through the entire selection, Woody would reappear in the kitchen with the same instrument every time: the red tambourine—firmly clenched in his jaw. Next he'd fall in line behind his two little bandmates and happily take up the rear for as long as the performance lasted.

At every age and stage, Steve and I tried to introduce our sons to the next level of music appreciation. We watched all the Disney musicals and listened to kids' tapes in the car. Steve and I sang "Itsy Bitsy Spider" and all the other timeless children's classics to the boys, peppering the mix with other classics like "Wake Up, Little Susie".

We sat through a series of Saturday morning cushion concerts put on by our community's symphony orchestra. Audience members brought cushions and pillows from home and sat on the floor while musicians taught bits of music theory by playing notes on lengths of garden hose and such. We soaked up an afternoon of Donny Osmond swirling and twirling in *Joseph and the Amazing Technicolor Dreamcoat*. On another evening, the percussive rhythms of the stage performance *STOMP* reverberated in our chests as the athletic musicians hammered, snapped, and brushed syncopated beats on garbage pails, playing cards, and brooms.

Some summer Saturday nights, in a cottage town on Lake Huron's shore, the four of us would fall in behind the Scottish pipe and drum band with hundreds of other parade watchers, and we would all march the length of the main street. At the halfway point, the musicians would put their instruments down in the parking lot of the local grocery store and let the kids bang on the drums and spit into the bagpipes while many of the band members had a smoke and got ready to march back down to the starting point.

While in preschool, Ted asked Santa for a piano. I tracked down the perfect little two-and-a-half-octave electric keyboard and had it stashed under the bed with weeks to spare. Then, two days before Christmas, Ted and I encountered Santa at a shopping mall. Ted, without flinching, hopped up onto the big guy's lap and carried on a lengthy conversation—just out of earshot.

"So," I asked Ted nervously when he returned, "what did you tell Santa you wanted him to bring?"

"A piano," Ted answered, to my relief. "And a monkey."

A monkey?

Christmas morning, Ted came upon a squat, stuffed gorilla (hastily purchased from the banana display at the corner grocery store the previous day), poised over his brand new little keyboard. That launched Ted's life-long interest in performance arts. A couple of years later, when we had been given Grandma's ornate and fairly well-tuned upright piano, Ted put on a Christmas concert in the living room, complete with a written program of the carols he'd be playing. He illustrated the cover with all sorts of Christmas symbols, and on the back cover he wrote out his biography for the audience.

Marshall gave piano lessons a shot, too, but he didn't like them, and we didn't make him continue. At the end of his Grade Five year, Steve and I gave him a junior acoustic guitar. Ted got a small number of golf clubs, a golf bag, and enough golf balls and tees to get him started. We could tell from the looks on their faces they thought we'd mixed up the gift tags. Marsh had a natural golf swing that challenged Steve's drives, and Ted was an avid musician. We assured them they had the gifts we'd intended. Marshall put his guitar in the back corner of his closet, and it sat there until he came home from camp later that summer. He'd met Nate the Great, his cabin counselor. Nate was handsome: tanned, buff, very cool, with long blond dreads. And Nate played guitar.

Marshall hauled his little acoustic out of his closet, signed up for guitar lessons at our local, small-town community center—two dollars a session—and was instantly bitten by a passion we hadn't seen before. In the coming years, driven solely by his love of the six-stringed instrument, Marshall easily logged the ten thousand hours it supposedly takes to become a master of anything.

The summer Marshall discovered his love of guitar, Ted bought a drum kit with his summer earnings from selling found golf balls. Then Ted bought an acoustic guitar, and Santa brought Marshall a starter electric—complete with a practice amp. After that, I lost count of the guitars they owned, now paid for with their summer job earnings. They formed a garage band in elementary school, wrote their own music, and performed locally throughout their high school years. Adult friends of ours would react in abject horror when they'd see our rec room crammed with drums and cymbals and amps and microphones and wires leading to guitars. We knew it wasn't the salvaged purple shag carpet they were reacting to.

"Are you nuts?" they'd ask Steve and me.

I never really understood what they meant until I went to one of the local talent shows and sat through

performances by mostly boy bands pounding out rendi-
tions of head-banging hard rock. Fortunately, that wasn't
Ted and Marshall's style, which tended toward the indie
blues and rock genre. I don't know how I'd have reacted if
they had been into heavy metal. As it was, our house was
a popular place for teens to hang out and make music.
We got to know our sons' friends, and we knew where
they were on a weekend night. And Steve and I enjoyed
the entertainment that drifted up from the basement.

In time, Ted joined a pipe and drum band and practiced
clarinet for the high school orchestra. Marshall played
tenor sax in the same orchestra, but his real love was still
the guitar.

Of course, not all of this had transpired as we sat on
our little beds at the Primrose Motel, but the fact we were
even there was a direct result of our desire to enrich our
sons' lives with culture.

The family I'd been raised in valued the appearance
of "culture" over almost anything. We combed our hair
before dinner, tipped our soup bowls to the back, and
everybody, including our cousins, knew to stand up
for Handel's "Hallelujah" chorus. We *certainly* would
not have insulted Julie Andrews, even in absentia,
with words like *mucus*. I felt offended or, at the very
least, excluded from the testosterone-based humor being enjoyed around me. Feeling slightly miffed, I sat up

straighter in my bed and took smaller bites of my Italian trio sandwich.

Since the others were not picking up on my physical cues, the spoofing in our motel room continued—escalated, actually. I'd never seen the song "Do-Re-Mi" acted out, and although I don't remember exactly what Steve, Ted, and Marshall improvised for "My Favorite Things," I can assure you they weren't schnitzel with noodles or anything tied up with string. I stuck my feet under the sheets and pulled the blankets up to my chest, my arms wrapped tightly around me.

"Edelweiss" was pure sacrilege; "Sixteen Going on Seventeen" almost blasphemous. By the time the von Trapps were singing "So Long, Farewell," I was in a snit. Not that I told anyone—it just felt like they'd spoiled my fun, and I felt left out of theirs.

I'd probably have done a better job of staying angry after the movie ended if it hadn't been for Steve. He started it. Right after he turned out the light on the little side table, he fell back into his twin bed. As his head hit the pillow, there was a loud thunk—and a soft moan.

"I think I found the phone book," he said, adding, with exquisite timing, "It's inside my pillow case."

Of course, it wasn't, but the visual image of what he'd just said started a case of uncontrollable giggling for Ted, Marshall, and me. Each wave of laughter dissolved a layer of the night's tension. We laughed louder and longer.

Finally, Steve called out in the dark, "Okay, everybody, that's it. It's time to get to sleep. We have an early start tomorrow."

That calmed things down—right until, again with perfect delivery and timing, Steve, copycatting the melody of the movie's closing tune, sang out with perfect pitch, "Good ni-i-ight." Ted and Marshall, picking up the cue immediately, echoed from their side of the room, "Good ni-i-ight."

"Oh, what the hell," I thought to myself. Belting out the final "Good ni-i-ight," typically off-key, I figured, "Julie will never know."

## ❦ Unique Talents

My lack of sense of direction means I get easily turned around in shopping malls. And then there's Wal-Mart, where the isles are separated by high shelving units and run only short lengths before changing direction. Is that not what a maze is? In contrast, Steve can drive directly to a place he visited once upon a time, long ago.

I'm good at other things, though. I can repeat the few Danish phrases I learned decades ago. My boyfriend at the time taught me a few niceties so that I could say something—*anything*—to his aunt, who was coming from Denmark.

I found it quite easy to memorize the phrases "How are you today?", "Thanks for dinner," and "You look very nice this evening," so next I worked on perfecting my Danish pronunciation. I sounded like the Swedish chef on *Sesame Street*. The night I was to meet *Moster* ("Aunt" in Danish), I ran my limited conversational bites past Frank's cousins out in the foyer before heading to the living room to meet her.

Both guys nodded in acceptance, if not approval, as I went through my list. I saved the longest sentence for last—one Frank described as a traditional Danish greeting that really had no English equivalent. It sounded like *"Passepore, passepore; elefenten sketeeska!"*

Frank's cousins snorted beer out of their noses. It

means "Watch out, watch out; the elephant's going to pee!"

The American developmental psychologist Howard Gardner, a professor at the Harvard Graduate School of Education, is well-known for his theory of multiple intelligences. He has identified nine types of intelligence: linguistic, logic-mathematical, musical, spatial, bodily-kinesthetic, interpersonal, intrapersonal, naturalistic, and existential.

Observe your kids and give them a chance to explore life in all these areas. You may be surprised to discover their abilities and strengths. Neither Steve nor I is talented in music. It turned out that both of our sons are.

## ❦ Manners for Live Performances

Teach your children the etiquette for attending live performances, whether at arts centers, school gyms, or community halls. Teach them these manners *before* you get to the concert or play. Tell them no one talks while a musician or actor is performing, and then demonstrate that to them. These are not pubs, bars, or coffeehouses. Next: Stay seated. If you arrive late or need to leave early, do so only between acts or musical pieces.

In all course corrections, remember to label your

child's *behavior*, not your child. And don't be afraid to be clear. Say things like "Talking while someone is performing is rude. We want to be polite, so we will not be talking during the performance. Wait and talk to me while people are clapping."

## 🌷Compliment Good Behavior

Congratulate your kids on good behavior. In fact, whenever you can, congratulate *anybody's* kids on good behavior out in public. Ask the parents, first, if you can talk to their children. Smile when you ask, or they're going to think you're weird. Tell the kids what you think they've done so well: listening quietly, using polite table manners—pick *anything*, wherever you are. The kids will look anything from pleased to uncomfortable, but if you take a good look at the parents' faces, you'll see that they are drinking in your praise like parched drill sergeants.

We all like to hear we're doing a good job, and nobody tells parents that.

## 🌷Sing with Your Kids

Sing with your kids—in the car, in the shower. Let them make up verses to silly tunes like "Down by the Bay." Improve their memories (and yours) with kids' songs like "There's a Hole in the Bucket" and "There's a Hole in the Bottom of the Sea." Many people have posted their versions on YouTube. Sing along with *them* if you don't know the words. Play opera on spaghetti night and "La Cucaracha" with tacos. (We kept an atlas on a pedestal in our kitchen nook so Ted and Marshall could see which country's food we were trying that night). It doesn't all have to be your favorite. As Ted and Marshall's Uncle Dave used to say, "There are only two kinds of music I don't like: country . . . and western."

## 🌱 Reward Hard Work

Steve and I chose to give Ted and Marshall some type of gift at the end of each school year to reward them for their hard work, good behavior, and excellent attendance. And we did this *before* report cards came out. We knew how hard they'd worked—not all the time or every day, but they were good students and good kids. Mind you, they were expected to be. Still, if you want good behavior from your kids, they need a *clear* understanding of the difference between the rewards and the consequences for how they choose to act.

These weren't bribes in the form of promised gifts for certain grade expectations, just family celebrations of a job well-done. Sometimes it was an evening out—pizza and a round of miniature golf—and at other times an actual gift. They didn't generally get identical presents. We always told them that to be fair, things don't have to be exactly the same.

## ❦ Making Choices

Ted and Marshall owned a *lot* of musical instruments. They purchased many themselves but Steve and I certainly bought a fair share of them. Acquiring them was expensive, even when we bought reconditioned or just plain used. As much as it may have appeared to some people that we were spoiling our kids with all these purchases, here's what we were thinking: all kids need a currency that is relevant in their culture. We wanted to respect their legitimate need to fit in and foster an interest that could lead to healthier, safer choices than, say . . . smoking.

## ❦ Learning to Be Flexible

Giving up my little snit fit over the *Sound of Music* mutiny was a conscious choice. Staying angry was pointless. It often serves us to be flexible; to break out of our predictable patterns of behavior and response. Just becoming aware of those patterns and habits can be enlightening. It's what allows us to examine them and test their relevance. It takes some self-awareness and some practice, but trying to observe our own proclivity to act a certain way can have some interesting benefits.

At our house, we have no claimed places at our dinner table. Anybody is welcome to sit anywhere. Just that degree of flexibility has afforded us many perks: a change of view; a fluid sense of who's at the "head" of the table each night, and the fact someone else's proximity to the kitchen means *he* can leap up to get the milk.

One Christmas morning, as Steve and I followed our routine preparations for cooking the turkey dinner, our ability to be flexible was tested on the spot. We discovered, to our horror, that our fresh turkey had gone bad. There is no mistaking what a turkey gone bad smells like.

I recognized it from my early teaching days in Waterloo. I shared an off-campus apartment with three young women. I was the working girl; they were university students. A group of university guys lived across the hall. It was the weekend of our Canadian Thanksgiving—the second Monday in October. The guys invited us to come over on Sunday for Thanksgiving dinner—that would be the day *after* the opening of Kitchener-Waterloo's Oktoberfest (or beerfest—depending on how you chose to celebrate). These four scholarly young men had done the math on a twenty-five-pound bird and realized it was going to have to go into the oven before noon. Since they already knew they'd still be in bed, sleeping off the previous night's festivities, they recalculated. The logic started with the idea that if it takes five hours to cook a turkey at 325 degrees Fahrenheit, they could simply cook it longer at a lower temperature. So, before they headed out for all the fun that can be had while wearing lederhosen, they set the oven dial at 200 degrees Fahrenheit and put the bird inside.

*Putrid* is how they described the smell that woke them early the next afternoon. Actually, once they opened their apartment door to cross the hall and explain that dinner was both literally and figuratively off, they didn't have to describe the smell to anyone on the fifth floor. Their reworking of the cooking chart had created the perfect petri dish for breeding salmonella—and anything else that smells.

So when Steve unwrapped our big fresh turkey that Christmas morning, we *knew*. The question was, now what? I'd already begun all the vegetables, because that's how we prepare turkey dinner at our house: I do all the veggies and gravy, Steve does the bird and the stuffing. We buy dessert.

Grandma, Uncle Dave, and his partner were all in the family room, dressed in their housecoats after an early morning of unwrapping presents. They were our houseguests, and they were expecting Christmas dinner. There were no stores open and no catering service to call at the last minute, so Steve and I headed to the freezer. Sorting through our limited provisions, it only took a few minutes to decide what to cook. Once we had figured out the menu, we spent the rest of the day hanging out with our guests, watching a new movie, and playing with Ted and Marshall and their new toys. What an unexpected treat it was to relax and enjoy one of the most special days of the year with our family.

Then, about half an hour before dinner, we headed to the kitchen and started the prep work. Our dinner was garlic shrimp pasta and Caesar salad. We so treasured that laid-back afternoon that Steve and I continued to serve garlic shrimp pasta for Christmas dinner for a number of years, shifting turkey to the day after—that is, until Grandma spoke up and insisted we revert to the long-standing tradition of turkey on December twenty-fifth. Another chance to be flexible.

## Garlic Shrimp Pasta

1 package spaghettini noodles
1/2 stick butter, melted
1/4 cup olive oil
2 tablespoons chopped fresh parsley
1/2 teaspoon salt

6 cloves garlic, crushed

1 pound raw black tiger shrimp

1 teaspoon grated lemon peel

1 tablespoon lemon juice

grated Parmesan cheese

Preheat oven to 400°F.

Prepare spaghettini according to package instructions.

Pour melted butter and olive oil into an oblong baking dish. Scatter bottom of pan with 1 tablespoon of the parsley, salt, and garlic. Arrange shrimp in a single layer. Bake 5 minutes, uncovered.

Turn shrimp and sprinkle with lemon peel, lemon juice, and the other tablespoon of parsley. Return to oven for 8–10 minutes more, or until shrimp are just tender.

Serve over cooked spaghettini topped with grated Parmesan cheese.

# CHAPTER 8

## *You Pick It Up*

THERE WERE OTHER ANIMALS BESIDES OUR FIRST DOG, SOLO, THAT we didn't keep: jars full of fireflies we captured among tall grasses on a hot July evening, or the baby bunny Steve found at the back of our house while he was out mowing the lawn. It had fallen into the shallow basement window well and couldn't get out.

Ted and Marshall named the little rabbit Jess and carried it around long enough for me to get in touch with the local Humane Society. We were assured that the proper thing to do was to put the bunny back on the lawn near the window well and wait for its mom to return. And she did. We got similar advice for the dazed little bird that had smacked its noggin into our back patio door. We made a warm nest of towels and left it in a low-sided cardboard lid on the back deck and kept an eye on it until it recovered its senses and flew off.

There was no question about us keeping the garter snake the boys uncovered beneath the boardwalk path at the cottage we were renting. They wanted to catch it but weren't exactly sure how to go about it, so I did it for them.

We always told our boys that the true measure of a person's character is how he or she behaves when no one is looking. That day on the beach, I had a different thought: the true measure of your character is how you behave when someone asks you to pick up a snake. After everyone had the chance to be brave enough to stroke it, we put it back where we had found it.

That was also the plan for the little green frog Marshall caught the day he and I were mucking around in the wetland behind our house—catch and release. I acquiesced, however, when he asked to keep it for one night so he could take it to kindergarten for show-and-tell (or bring-and-brag, as some teachers I worked with used to call it). We put that little frog in a small aquarium with twigs, mud, grass, and leaves, and because we couldn't find any sort of screen, we set a small pane of glass on top, leaving just enough space for air to get in—and apparently, for a little frog to get out.

I should have known better. Exactly the same thing happened to me as a young teacher. Our custodian was desperate to find a new home for two hamsters. He hadn't thought to consult his wife before he'd brought rodents home as pets for their five-year-old son. Hamsters looked like mice to her, and it turned out they weren't going to be keeping any at their house.

"They're both females," Mr. Hangartner assured me as

he placed the newcomers to my Grade Two class on the windowsill that ran the full length of the classroom, "so they do just fine together in this cage." Well, it wasn't a cage; it was an aquarium with a glass lid that he set off to the edge just enough to let in some air.

Only one of the two females escaped. Our class discovered she was missing one Monday morning when I was explaining homonyms, like *flour* and *flower*. "The first you bake with, the second is like our geranium," I explained, pointing to the pot on the windowsill—the one near the aquarium. The pot was still there, but the geranium was missing.

I guess if one hamster stands on another hamster, she can clamber out of an aquarium, but her pal gets left behind. And I guess hungry hamsters eat geraniums.

It turned out those little rodents were more than just pals. The escapee gave birth to an entire litter of baby hamsters in behind a built-in bookcase at the front of the classroom. How *do* you tell the sex of a hamster?

The night of open house for parents that year, our room was by far the most popular. Everyone wanted to come and see what was in Ms. Parsons' class. I had supervised as the kids built a little corral around the opening under the bookcase. We kept water and food available to the mother hamster as she came and went. Every now and then a few of the babies would waddle forth, giving the visitors a chance to *ooh* and *aah*.

Strategies had been discussed in the staff room. I couldn't just catch the mom—the babies would starve behind the bookcase, and we couldn't simply pluck up each of the babies as it appeared; they were nursing, so they'd still starve. My plan was to wait it out and see what could be accomplished when all the critters were big enough to fend for themselves. In the meantime, at random, the tiny family would appear on the linoleum underneath my chalkboard, and my spelling lessons would go straight to hell in a handbasket. Who can compete with furry little faces with tiny silken ears and coal-black eyes?

So when Marshall discovered there was no frog in the aquarium, we put out flat dishes of water and—well, flat dishes of water, because we didn't know what to feed a frog, really.

We watched and hunted for that tiny amphibian for days. Weeks.

I finally found it. Normally, when we've lived in a house long enough that I think it must be time to clean underneath the appliances, we move instead. Write the appliances into the offer of sale and avoid cleaning underneath them; that's my homemaker's tip.

I'm kidding, but only barely. So when spring cleaning rolled around (I can't guarantee it was the *next* spring), I found that little frog. He was flat on his back, mummified and swaddled in dust bunnies, under the stove.

We didn't keep the pair of rosy-cheeked baby cockatiels, either, and that was very sad for all of us. Santa had brought them to Ted and Marshall. There they were, beside the tree in a tall green cage outfitted with toys, food, and water. Their tiny feathers were glossy, with iridescent-jewel tones. Our boys were ecstatic. You can teach young cockatiels to talk, and Ted and Marshall made big plans. It took a few weeks, but the little birds were just beginning to gain confidence in stepping onto an offered finger when I discovered I was terribly allergic to them. I had just finished having chemotherapy and radiation for breast cancer in mid-December, and I suspect my immune system was at an all-time low, but those little fledglings had me sneezing and weeping and sniffing all day long.

I think I was just too sad, or maybe feeling too guilty, to be the one to break the news to our boys. Steve did the dirty work. He reported back to me after their talk that it was touch and go for a while as to who would have to leave—the birds or me—but in the end, I took Patches and Polly back to the breeders so they could find a new home.

Our family went all kinds of places to check out new creatures. We visited the Toronto Zoo. Closer to home, there was a terrific pet shop at the other end of our city.

The staff used to bring domestic and exotic varieties out for children to take a closer look. Marshall became convinced he wanted some type of reptile, but I said no, we wouldn't be getting an animal to which we had to feed other live animals. We drove through the countryside on a regional farm tour and met dairy cattle and emus. We went to the petting barn at a spring festival just outside the city limits.

It was there we came to appreciate the benefits of learning animal jargon at a young age. The long Quonset hut that housed the farm animals was beginning to fill up, and it was getting harder for the four of us to stick together, so I took Marshall and headed for the sheep pen. Steve, with Ted in tow, headed over to see the massive workhorses. We agreed we'd all meet up somewhere in the middle.

That happened sooner than later, since a short, wiry woman dressed in jeans and a flannel shirt came into the barn and began moving people off to the circumference, explaining as she went that the farrier, or blacksmith, was coming, and there was going to be a demonstration. They'd be bringing one of the big horses out, so everyone needed to step back and make room.

This sounded like great fun to me. I understood this meant our boys would have the chance to see a horse get its hooves trimmed and filed and new shoes forged to fit, so Marshall and I scurried around to meet up with Steve and Ted, just as the farrier's assistant was leading a big, steady, old Percheron out of its stall toward a leather-aproned man. A specialized kind of tool kit sat open on the floor at his feet. We watched from the outer ring as the farrier ran his strong hands down the back of the mare's front left leg; she politely lifted her hoof, and the farrier deftly captured and held it between his knees. As he began the work of pulling off the old shoe, Steve yanked me back a distance and whispered, "See that woman?"

It could have been the one from the parking lot. Her back was to me, and I had to stand on tiptoe to catch a glimpse, but the sweep of her honey-toned hair and the diamond stud earrings looked familiar. Anyway, even from the shoulders up, she didn't look like the type to be hanging out at a barn.

Steve could barely contain himself to tell the story. He'd been moving backward, with Ted, according to the instructions of the farrier's wiry little female helper, when the elegant woman ahead of us had appeared in a flash from across the Quonset hut. Grabbing her husband's arm, she practically yelled at him, "Honey, we need to get out of here now!"

Bewildered, the man turned to his visibly upset partner and asked, "Why?"

"Because," she wailed, "they're going to shoot a horse!"

Steve described the man's response as sounding fairly well practiced, as though this sort of thing happened to him a *lot*.

"No, darling," the man said, shaking his head. Taking her upper arms gently in his hands, he turned her to face him. Calmly, he enunciated, "*Shoe*, sweetheart. They're going to *shoe* the horse."

## ❦ Character

The true measure of our character *is* how we behave when no one is looking.

## ❦ Don't Be Scared

Perhaps, as you head out into the wilds of a local wetland or nature preserve, it will be a comfort to you to differentiate between two human responses. Unless they are venomous, snakes do not have to scare you. Generally, they are small and harmless. They'll *startle* you, but that's different. Teach your children the difference, too.

## ❦ Snakes

The first time I saw a snake, it was winding its way across the warm sand—between my *feet*. I wasn't the first kid to spot it (because my head was up and I was looking at something else), but the kid who did spot it screamed. So I screamed, then everybody was screaming, so of course I thought snakes were very scary—even the little garter type I encountered that day at the grassy edge of a beach.

The second time I saw a snake was at the St. Louis Zoo. A handler had an enormous python out for viewing—and touching. Most of its length was draped lazily over the lower branches of a tree, but its head was being supported by the man in the zoo uniform. Figuring the man had control of the business end of the snake, I sucked up my courage and stepped forward to touch the reptile somewhere more along its middle.

I'd say that section of the snake was about the same circumference as my thigh, but I think I mean the circumference of my thigh that day when I was twenty-two years old. Anyway, it wasn't a slithery size, so I didn't really think the animal would whip around and latch onto me if I touched it. It looked too fat and lazy to bother.

It felt like a handbag: dry and solid yet supple. It was muscular—kind of like my thigh but scalier and cooler.

When Ted and Marshall were still quite little, they had three girl friends who lived up the street—sisters. They were *petrified* of spiders. Their *mother* was petrified of spiders. All the neighbors knew when any of them encountered any type or size of arachnid on their back deck or front porch, because one of them would start screaming and then they'd all start screaming.

I had a good idea of what to expect when I picked up that little garter snake for Ted and Marshall, but I still had to suck up my courage to do it. It wasn't the first thing I felt like doing, but the last thing I felt like doing was making them afraid of a little snake.

## ❦ Don't Look

For those of you who are classroom teachers, I pass along this story.

Two little boys are bringing up the rear of a ragtag line of Grade Two kids out on a field trip with their teacher. The rest of the group is farther ahead on the woodlot path when a little brown rabbit hops out from among the trees and stops directly in the path of the two youngsters.

"Hey!" cries the first. "Look at the bunny!"

"Duh!" snaps his little friend. *"Don't* look at the bunny, or you'll have to write a story about it!"

## ❦ Nature Smart

One of the multiple intelligences identified by Howard Gardner is naturalist intelligence. Allowing your kids the chance to relate to nature provides those whose strengths lie in this area a very different "curriculum" from the one that is geared toward those whose abilities lie in the more traditionally accepted areas of intelligence. Gardner also reminds us that there are many ways for children to demonstrate understanding in their areas of strength. So, teachers... maybe they don't always have to write a story about what they've experienced.

## ❦ Love of Animals

Marshall was keenly interested in all things animal kingdom. We made regular trips to our local library, seeking books and videos on cheetahs and orcas and wolves and such. We read and watched and learned about habitats and migration routes, and while we were doing this, Marshall came to really care about these animals. So, when he was in Grade One, he self-published (by that I mean he sat down with paper, pencil, crayons, and a stapler) an entire series of booklets on endangered species. Then he set up a table on our lawn—the same one he and Ted had used the day they sold lemonade to our neighbors for a net loss of $13.87—and he sold his booklets to the kind people who lived on our street.

We sent that money to the World Wildlife Foundation with a letter explaining where the proceeds had come from. They sent him back a very nice letter and a membership card.

## ❦ What Became of the Hamsters

The hamsters survived and went to good homes. I found them all early one morning under the classroom sink. I guess they'd gone exploring through the night, following one another. Like little tightrope walkers they'd obviously been trying to balance along the top rims of the tall empty apple juice cans our class used for art class. Maybe it was like dominos, but each one fell into a can, and they were rattling around under the sink when I arrived to prepare my classes.

I went and got Mr. Hangartner; after all, he started the whole thing. He emptied all the little rodents into one big bin. We set down food and water, and I went to the copying machine to make duplicates of a flyer to be sent home with each kid in my class: FREE TO A GOOD HOME.

## 𝗪 Our Dear Woody

Creating opportunities to interact with and care for animals in our family has been an enriching experience for us all. Learning to be good stewards to animals you bring into your home is a both a moral responsibility and an inexpressible blessing. Just as in our role as parents, we can't be flawless in our care, but we can try.

When we weren't paying close enough attention, Woody got hit by a car on the highway at the end of our quiet lane. He lived, but he needed extensive surgery to allow him to walk—and run in a lopsided way—after that. As he aged, arthritis set in. And his heart enlarged, creating some breathing difficulties. So, just as we had done many years before with Ted's Precious Lambie, we sought the best care for our dear old Lab. He got acupuncture, laser therapy, and seasonal injections designed to ease the stiffness in his joints.

Until just beyond his fifteenth birthday, Woody trotted after one or more of us as we led him into the woods behind our property for his daily walks. True to his character, he rarely took the beaten path we took. Rather, that feisty old boy would lower his head and push his way through all manner of obstacles to uncharted territory where the smells were the richest and life could offer something delectably new—a lesson we try to remember.

On a September morning, when Ted was away at university, Woody woke up having difficulty breathing.

Years before, out of the necessity to prepare myself for this day, I had begun having conversations with our loving vet. "How will we know the day has come?" I asked. "What can we do with his body?"

The day had come.

Woody died peacefully in my arms at the vet's office. We wrapped his body in the soft blue sheet I had bought, laundered, ironed, and put away in preparation long ago.

We buried Woody among the apple trees on our vet's farm, on the crest of the hill that overlooks the bay. Steve and Marshall dug his grave. Our vet tenderly arranged his body in the pose of a dog at rest, and we said goodbye to the form in which we had all come to know and love that wonderful dog.

Every now and then, even still, Woody romps through our hearts and our memories, and, as he always did, he makes us laugh.

# CHAPTER 9

## *The Hacketts of Tampa*

THE YEAR MARSHALL WAS IN GRADE FIVE, HE WROTE A SPEECH
on his first canoeing trip at Camp Wabanaki. It was very
well received, especially by his classmates who loved the
part about the kid throwing up in the tent. In Grade Six,
Marshall had even better material to work with: folks I'll
call the Hacketts of Tampa.

Steve and I had decided to take Ted and Marshall on
an adventure to Sanibel Island, Florida, that year. The
beach there is renowned for its seashells, and sometimes
dolphins play right at the shore.

The morning of our scheduled departure, the airline
we'd booked with declared bankruptcy.

Our bags were packed, Woody was ensconced at the
dog sitter's with a week's worth of kibble, and the gulf
island was calling to us. There were other options but
promising to make the best of the situation, we packed
everything, including a tiny TV-VCR that ran off a
cigarette-lighter power source and about a month's
supply of videos, into our relatively new van and
drove off.

We had a wonderful time. Right until it was time to come home.

It was still dark the Friday morning we packed up to start the long drive back. An armadillo was nosing around the resort garden as we rolled quietly away, not wanting to awaken the neighbors who were still asleep. Steve had a deadline for being back in Ontario: a five-day workshop he was scheduled to conduct beginning the next Monday.

He took the first shift behind the wheel, and the boys and I drifted off to sleep. I woke as I felt the vehicle roll to a stop. Figuring Steve must be tired, and readying myself to take over, I shook myself awake.

*Odd spot for a driver change,* I remember thinking as I looked around. We'd come to rest on the shoulder of a multilane interstate highway on the edge of Tampa. The get-to-work-by-nine commuter crowd was whizzing past our door handles, leaving zero room to hop out and make the switch.

"You okay?" I asked.

"No." Steve's response was tense. "The van just died."

"What do you mean, 'died'?" I prodded.

"I don't know." Steve looked baffled. "We just lost power." He'd negotiated three lanes of traffic with just enough time to allow us to come to a halt somewhere other than the center of the expressway.

We *had* a cell phone but this was the year 2002 and you could use a cell phone for little more than calling directory assistance. Sitting on the side of a Florida highway, we had no idea who to call. So we sat. State troopers passed us. Thousands of people passed us. In desperation, we hung a white pillowcase from the rear window. Many more people whizzed past. Then a very nice man backed his car skillfully along the shoulder. I went to his passenger window. That's when I learned about call boxes. The closest one was not too far behind our broken-down van. All I had to do was go, pick up the receiver, and the next in line of a lottery of tow truck operators would be there, on the other end of the phone, prepared to come to our rescue.

That's how we came to meet Mr. Hackett. With our introduction to him also came the first of many opportunities that day to reinforce this lesson for our boys: don't stare.

Certainly, Mr. Hackett was a nice enough man. He was polite and hospitable, but to say he was a disadvantaged person would be a gross understatement. I felt sorry for him. A lifelong lack of dental care likely explained his gapped smile, but I thought Mr. Hackett could have made a little more effort on the hygiene front. Any recent attempt at bathing would have been appreciated by those of us riding in his truck with him. His yellowed toenails made a real impression on Marshall—especially the way they curled upward out of his sandals. I remember wondering, with a sense of problems ahead, *Do real mechanics wear sandals? Even in Florida?*

As he hooked our two vehicles together, Mr. Hackett gave us a choice. Did we want him to tow our van all the way across the city of Tampa to our brand of dealership, or did we want him to simply tow us to his garage, which was just down the road a piece?

We opted for Mr. Hackett's nearby location, hoping for a quick fix, so we could get back on the road in good time. Perhaps if we'd had just a little more information, Steve and I would have gone for option two.

As we pulled into Mr. Hackett's yard, in a district where lots of other disadvantaged people lived, Steve and I exchanged a look of alarm. Cars and parts of cars were heaped everywhere. Rust had taken over long ago. The entire operation was in a state of near collapse.

"Follow me," Mr. Hackett invited us, as he led the way into the office. Mounds of aging paperwork were heaped on the lone desk. An adding machine was the most current piece of technological equipment we could see. Everything wore a look of destitution and neglect. There were no waiting room chairs, so the boys and I settled onto the torn-out, soiled seats from a vintage automobile that rested against the wall. The dusty concrete floor was cool under our feet.

"Don't touch *anything!*" I instructed our sons.

I tried to eavesdrop on the conversation Steve was having with Mr. Hackett, but the hum of the vending machine drowned out the specifics. Steve relayed to me later that Mr. Hackett was just the business operator and tow truck responder; somebody else was the mechanic. That sounded reassuring.

But the mechanic was going to be a little late getting to work that day, Mr. Hackett warned. He'd lost his license for DUI charges and hadn't yet found a lift to work.

"DUI?" I asked Steve.

"Driving under the influence," he explained tersely.

*Great*, I thought, *what next?*

Well, it turns out that what happened next was not much of anything. The mechanic, who finally made it in and spent considerable time with his head under the hood, needed a little more time, he said, before he could tell us what was wrong with our van.

"How much time?" Steve pressed him.

"See," here he seemed to be considering how to tell us the next part. "what I need is a manual for your make and model of van."

He didn't have such a manual, but he knew a guy who had a place not far from there who did have one. So he and Mr. Hackett were just going to tow our van to that garage and see if they could figure out from the manual what was wrong with the engine.

To this day, I cannot tell you why we said, "Okay."

We had already spent a very long time sitting on the torn-out seats, reading the notices pinned to the wall, and trying not to touch anything or stare at the staff. Our boys were old enough to have figured out their mother had a generally irreverent, often politically incorrect sense of humor. I couldn't resist expanding on the fears they were beginning to have.

More than once, they had asked the very nice and equally disadvantaged lady who was working in the office (most likely Mrs. Hackett) for change for the vending machine. The day was heating up and we had no food with us, so we were using frequent sips of cool beverages to quash our appetites.

With each request, this helpful woman would shuffle off somewhere in her flowered housedress and be gone for a very long time. Always, she would reemerge with precise change for one buck at a time.

"Doesn't it seem suspicious that a business would have no cash?" Marshall whispered. "Shouldn't they have *some* money?"

"Marshall," I told him, "we are probably the only business that has come through these doors in months. No, years. The Hacketts have likely already sold our van,

leaving us stranded here in their waiting room, somewhere on the outskirts of Tampa. Next they'll be coming for the children!" The three of us dissolved in a fit of
infectious giggles.

"Where could we get something to eat?" Steve asked
the woman shuffling the paperwork.

*How can you ask that question here?* I wondered. I
was prepared to eat my own foot before contemplating
what a meal with the Hacketts might entail should we
end up eating someplace with them.

But, contrary to my darkest fears, that question elic-
ited the gracious demonstration of hospitality for which
Americans on their home soil are known. Some other
person who just happened to be at Mr. Hackett's that
afternoon ushered us into his massive old Cadillac, and
he drove us to the spot (most likely the only spot) way,
way down the road where we could order lunch. And
practice not staring.

"This is a carnie town," our driver explained. The tilt of
my head and the arch of my eyebrows prompted him to
continue. "These are circus folk. The whole area. This is
where they live when they're not on the road."

That went a long way in explaining the clientele—
like the decidedly senior woman in the booth behind
Steve. Despite her sagging and wrinkled features she
was dressed and made-up as if waiting in the wings for

her turn on the trapeze. I decided I could ease up on our enforcement of the don't-stare rule.

So our family had a nice lunch of freshly made bacon, lettuce, and tomato sandwiches with all those interesting people. We paid for our driver's sandwich and were then given a lift back to the garage. To our relief, our van was in the parking lot. To our dismay, it was still hooked on to the back of the tow truck.

"Tell you what," Steve suggested amiably to Mr. Hackett. "How about if we go for option two?"

So, at 4:45 that Friday afternoon, Mr. Hackett unhooked our van in front of a pristine service bay far across the city, pocketed too much money for the services he'd been unable to provide, and said a friendly goodbye.

The service manager for that dealership had agreed on the phone to meet us. Just seeing his crisply laundered uniform and his laced-up leather shoes, as he walked us through the waiting room to his tidy office, made me feel better. So did the sight of upholstered chairs and a laptop computer.

He had popped the hood of the van when we arrived, and with remarkable speed and the assistance of a small piece of modern diagnostic technology sprouting many wires, declared unequivocally, "It's your transmission."

"So?" Steve queried.

"So that's going to take some time to fix," the manager offered.

"How much time?" The question rang an echo in my head.

"Well," he replied, "it's nearly quitting time. We won't be able to get at it today."

*That sounds reasonable*, I was thinking.

He continued, "And wouldn't you know, there are only three days a year we're closed other than Sundays: Christmas, Thanksgiving, and tomorrow, when we're taking inventory. I can already tell you, though, the closest transmission to fit your vehicle," he paused and looked up from the screen of his computer, "is in Georgia. It will take some time to get it here on one of our delivery trucks."

Steve's head fell back, and he was silent. "Okay," he finally said, breathing deeply, "is there a faster way to get it here?"

I love this guy. Just when everything is going from bad to worse, he believes there can be a better solution.

"Well, you could have it FedExed," the manager offered, "but that would cost you. And it's too late now to place the order. It'll have to wait until Monday."

Monday? Steve needed to be in Ontario on Monday to conduct a five-day workshop! I recognized the look he was giving me at that moment. It was kind of like the one he wore when I went into labor. It said, "I really wish I could do this for you, honey, but—"

So we gave the go-ahead for the FedEx delivery, shook hands with the service manager, told him how much we appreciated the loaner car he'd arranged for us, and went off to make a new plan.

First, we rented a unit at a Country Inn and Suites nearby. That gave us a tiny kitchen in which to prepare meals in the coming days. Next, Steve booked a flight out of Tampa for the following day. Then we decided to take some of the pressure off and go out to have some fun. Dinner at a family restaurant was followed by a movie at the theater. I know it was *Monsters, Inc.*, but I don't remember much about the plot. I was sitting in the dark contemplating my own nightmare: the twenty-four hours of driving that lay ahead with nobody to relieve me.

Saturday morning, we were all making preparations to take Steve to the airport when I discovered I didn't have my purse. Backtracking the events of the previous night, I could remember hanging it on the arm of my theater seat just as the previews began to roll. Panic rose in my chest. Steve was leaving and I didn't have my driver's license, a credit card, or my debit card to pay for gas, meals, and accommodations.

There are lots of honest people in Tampa. It turns out some of them go to family movies and some of them work in cinema offices. After a quick return to the theater, I had my purse back with all its contents. For a short time, that cheered me right up—until the boys and I walked with Steve as far into the labyrinth of airport security as we were permitted. Ted and Marshall gave their dad a goodbye hug and kiss. I did the same.

"Everything will be just fine," Steve assured me.

"I know," I replied stoically. We kissed again; then I watched him turn and walk away.

"Wait right here," I told our sons. "I just need a quick comfort stop."

The ladies' room was empty, a quick scan for feet in each stall revealed. I pushed open the door to the end cubicle, sat down fully clothed on the toilet, and sobbed into a wadded ball of bathroom tissue.

I was so afraid. It's not that I'm not a good driver; I am. It's not that I hadn't driven that route before; I had a number of times with my female teacher friends when we drove to Daytona Beach for March break.

It wasn't that I didn't have a good sense of direction; well, actually, that's not true. I don't have a good sense of direction at all. Steve is surprised I make it home for dinner every night; he says I could get lost in a paper bag.

But that's not what scared me. I'd never traveled such a distance before, being solely responsible for the safety of our sons. What if something happened?

So sitting on the toilet, I summoned my instincts and my intellect and came up with a plan that made me feel better. More confident now, I splashed some cold water on my face and went out to collect the boys.

Since there was nothing to be accomplished on Sunday, Ted, Marshall, and I piled into the loaner car and headed to the interior of the state—to Universal Studios in Orlando, where I got to refine being scared by going upside down and backward in the dark at high speed all day long.

Monday, I confirmed that our transmission was on its way. Tuesday, the work was complete, and the three of us were gratefully on our way by late afternoon.

*Dear Lord*, I prayed, making the supplication in my head before I slid the controls into drive, *please help us arrive safely at our next stop.*

That was the plan I had come up with to help settle my nerves. Every time I turned the key in the ignition, starting the next leg of our journey, that's what I said—even if we'd only stopped at a Cracker Barrel roadside restaurant to pee. I figured you couldn't ask a divine source for safe arrival and then drive like an idiot. What kind of God would support an arrangement like that? So my frequent prayers were my conscious reminder that I needed to stay focused.

We arrived in Georgia, far enough out of the hills of the

South to avoid the customary early morning fog, which would have made Wednesday's start challenging, and we tucked in for the night.

Our goal for Wednesday was to make it to Ohio. It turned out that a lot of other people had exactly the same thought. This was the day before the U.S. Thanksgiving. Apparently, everybody in the country goes home for Thanksgiving. Surely there must be some who fly, but that year, it seemed they were all driving. And they all seemed to be going to Ohio, and they were all in a big hurry.

As much as I could, the entire day I encouraged our boys to feed one movie after another into the little TV in the backseat. It kept their focus inside our van. Outside were more crashes and rollovers than I'd ever seen. Traffic came to a complete standstill many times as emergency workers tried to clear the wreckage.

"Look at that beautiful landscape," I'd say, drawing the boys' attention to some feature outside their windows as the movie credits rolled and the entertainment ended, pointing them in the opposite direction from the carnage we were passing in the adjacent lanes.

We finally made it to Ohio. As we had done the night before, we unplugged the little TV and took it with us into the hotel room, not wanting to entice someone to break into our vehicle. The next morning I was the one who carried it back to the van. Figuring it couldn't be too difficult to sort out what plug went into which hole, I attempted to hook it up.

There were a decidedly limited number of combinations and permutations to the inputs and outputs, yet I chose the one that blew the fuse in the little TV. We were still more than ten hours from home, and there were still movies Marshall and Ted hadn't watched yet. Our first mission that Thursday was to go buy a new fuse.

Except it was Thanksgiving. Unable to find a place that was open that also sold TV fuses, we merged with the northbound traffic on I-75 again and began the first of many, many silly car games.

In Detroit there is an exit from the interstate highway to the Ambassador Bridge to Canada that comes up very fast on your right. If you miss it and take the turn I did, you wind up in an unsavory area of the city. That's how my grandmother would have described where we found ourselves: *unsavory*. I had the impression of having inadvertently arrived on a massive, monochromatic movie set. All the businesses were closed, the buildings abandoned. The traffic signals worked, but their changing colors provided the only animation. The whole place was eerily devoid of life. Ours was the only vehicle on the long four-lane road.

"Guys," I sounded the alert. "I missed our turn. Look for signs to the bridge to Canada."

Ahead, on the right, Ted spotted a group of six or seven figures, huddled on a corner. As we rolled forward, they came into focus. *Unsavory* is what my grandmother would have called the whole lot of them, but what I saw was a bunch of disadvantaged men huddled together against the raw November wind. I don't think they were on a coffee break from work.

"Mom, why don't you stop and ask one of those guys for directions?" Ted suggested.

Feeling very uncomfortable with the glances some of the men were shooting our way, I hugged the center line as we passed through the intersection on a well-timed green light, and said, optimistically, "Nah. Come on; it's a great big bridge, and it's around here somewhere. How hard can it be to find?"

And suddenly, there it was. And there was the sign with an arrow pointing us in the right direction. I paid the toll and we crossed the bridge.

Having cleared the border, I made a quick decision. It was an easy one. Rather than drive five hours to get home, I'd drive for just another two and check in with Steve at his hotel in London, Ontario. If we made good time, the boys and I could arrive before he finished up the day's workshop, and we'd surprise him.

The hotel staff knew us and provided a key. A sudden weariness washed over me as we waited in the lobby for the elevator. As the doors slid open, and we hit the button for the twenty-second floor, Ted perked up.

"What if we go into Dad's room and find all kinds of spy stuff?" he asked. "What if he actually isn't a business consultant after all? You know, like Arnold Schwarzenegger in True Lies."

I love that movie: Jamie Lee Curtis transforming herself in front of that hotel hallway mirror; her revisionist makeover of the little black dress; and what she does with the water from the flower vase. Brilliant—from Susie Homemaker to scandalous vamp in under half a minute.

My reverie was cut short by Marshall's question. "What if we go in there and find there's another woman in his room?" he gasped.

The events of the past six days had honed my response to exactly this kind of unexpected challenge to a razor-edged sharpness. Nothing could throw me now. Drawing myself up to my full height, I took a deep breath and answered Marshall with the full confidence demonstrated by Jamie Lee Curtis's character, Doris.

"Not a problem," I assured him. "I'll just have to kill her."

## 🎺 Give Them a Map

Whenever we traveled, I would give our guys a map and show them our route. That way, they had a good sense of what the answer would be to the question "Are we there yet?"

## 🎺 Watching TV

Steve and I didn't spend a lot of time discussing guidelines for movie watching, TV viewing, video game selection, or the amount of time we'd allow Ted and Marshall to spend engaged in any of these. Nor did we spend a lot of time discussing age appropriateness for what they'd see. We didn't spend a lot of time because coming to an agreement on what our rules would be was quick and easy: our kids should spend most of their time at play or, possibly, reading. They had many years ahead of them to watch adult content but very few years to delight in the simple pleasures of kid flicks, and no one would be bringing video games into our home in which the objective was to hunt down and kill people. That final rule applied even to their friends and even into their teen years.

A refinement of the rules was this: you can only do one thing at a time. So even when they were little and *Sesame Street* was on TV, Ted and Marshall knew that if they wanted to watch it, they had to sit empty-handed and focus their attention on it. (Well, snacks were allowed on the couch.) If they lost interest before the end of a program, the TV was turned off.

Initially, this meant watching just a segment of a show in direct proportion to their attention span. But that's what we, as parents, were working to develop: their attention spans and their ability to focus on one thing. TV did not run in the background while the boys played in the same room with toys. Playing was one thing and watching TV was another. They had to choose.

In contrast they had playmates who in the middle of a Disney flick would slide off the sofa, distracted by some impulse, to amuse themselves at the toy table. Then they'd rejoin Ted and Marshall for another portion of the movie. Sometimes they'd even try to engage our boys in conversation, which didn't go over all that well, given that it interrupted the plot and the dialogue.

The cautions here are twofold. First, research has shown multitasking to have adverse effects on speed, accuracy, quality of output, and energy consumption. This applies to adults and kids alike. Give your child the advantage of learning to stay focused on one thing at a time.

Second, unmonitored TV watching can become your

child's aimless way of self-parenting. If no one is available to be actively engaged with the child, if there is no other creative and stimulating activity to choose, TV is an alarmingly available substitute to a child who's been instructed in how to operate the remote. And as we all know, there are some unsavory role models for them to discover as they flip channels.

Having said all that, I can't explain how our sons ended up watching *True Lies* at the age they did. It was originally released as an R-rated movie, listed for its "action/violence and some language."

Actually, I *can* explain: they saw it at home, with (you guessed it) us—Steve and me, their oh-so-vigilant parents. Both Steve and I thought it terrifically funny; a super plot acted out in comic book fashion. Pow! Blam! Boom!

Ted and Marshall thought it was terrifically funny, too—so much so that we even took it to family camp, where the tweens watched it in the dining hall the night of the big sleepover. On the dock, the next morning, one of the moms was fuming. "I can't believe someone would think that was appropriate," she steamed. "We would *never* have let our son see that movie."

I was caught off guard. I'd have guessed that the two of us shared similar values when it came to censoring what our boys watched, so I sort of shrugged off the criticism, thinking maybe she and her husband were actually even stricter than Steve and I were. And I kept thinking that until the next time I watched the movie.

"Some language"? How about the f-bomb? The movie offers up everything from traffic violations to seduction, torture, destruction of public and private property on a massive scale, infidelity, prostitution, shooting and killing, lying, theft, kidnapping, and, oh, references to oral sex.

How did we miss that and see only the funny bits? Anyway, I apologize to the family camp crowd.

## Time Alone Downstairs

One of our pediatrician's most welcomed suggestions actually allowed for unsupervised TV watching. It was no mistake that Ted's nickname as a little kid was Rooster, since he woke up as early as he did. At a regular checkup appointment, I voiced it as a complaint to the doctor.

"Well," he advised, "give yourselves a break on the weekends." And he went on to describe what he meant.

I could hardly wait.

We got Ted a little digital clock for his bedside table. "When you wake up tomorrow morning, you can go downstairs as long as this first number says seven," we instructed him that Friday night, and we taped a little tented card onto the top of the clock with the numeral 7 printed clearly on it.

There were three rules: no touching the stove, no going outside, and have fun.

We had shown him how to hit just the power button on the remote control; the channel was preprogrammed for Saturday morning cartoons. A bowl of dry cereal sat waiting, next to the remote, on the coffee table, and a sippy cup of apple juice was on a refrigerator shelf where he could retrieve it without knocking things over. And just in case he might feel lonely, I set his big stuffed bear up on the couch with his own bowl of cereal.

Thinking there was a chance the remote might not work or that Ted would tire of what was on TV (not likely on a Saturday morning, but I've always been big on contingency plans and sleeping in), before we went to bed on weekend nights Steve and I would also arrange what Ted came to call setups in the area behind the sofa. Using odd combinations that would offer a jumping-off point for further play for Ted (and, of course, Marshall, when he was old enough to make it down the stairs with his big brother), Steve and I would create wacky vignettes from the toy table.

Captain Hook might be plopped into the driver's seat of a dump truck loaded with plastic french fries, its course set for a wooden tower of blocks linked by a bridge to the bright yellow train track where a herd of farm animals blocked the way of the engine as it emerged from the tunnel.

The plush yellow giraffe puppet was being dragged into a cardboard box by the fat brown gorilla, and both were being chased by cowboys on horseback.

These were just something to get them started with a new idea. This time alone downstairs was one of our boys' first big steps towards independence.

## ❦Time's Up!

As the time approaches to leave a venue or a play-date, give your kids reliable, *accurate* warnings that the time to pack up is approaching. Start at the fifteen-minute mark (unless you've been at something all day—then you could give them a heads-up when departure time is one hour away), then let them know again when ten minutes remain. At the five-minute mark, suggest they fit in the last thing they want to accomplish. Warn them at two minutes and, finally, at the last minute remaining. When that's up, don't negotiate. With repetition, over time, your kids will learn two things: you're serious when you say time's up, and how to gauge the passage of fifteen minutes.

## ❦Swearing

Despite the occasional lapse in judgment on other things, Steve and I chose to not swear in front of our sons—no *damn*, no *hell*. After many years, we introduced the occasional *crap*, to their surprise. As they got older, we explained that the choice to swear or not swear was theirs to make, but it should never happen within earshot of an adult. They knew we swore (gasp) in the company of some friends, but we did not swear around them, and certainly never *at* them.

But then there was a certain day. They were in their early teens by then. Brian and Kevin, their lifelong friends, had come north to spend the weekend. I'd already called downstairs with the ten-minute warning to tidy up and collect all the gear so we could make the hour-and-a-half drive to meet up with Brian and Kevin's mom.

So when I arrived in the rec room nine minutes later to find all four of them still absorbed in a video game, I wasn't happy, but I was *really* not happy about the explosion of plates and glasses and napkins and pizza boxes from the night before. The mess spread across the coffee table and spilled onto the floor.

"What the hell were you thinking?!" I barked. "Get this cleaned up now!" And I stomped upstairs.

That's where Ted confronted me. "Mom," he said, "I know you're upset about the mess, and we're going to clean it up, but why would you swear at us?"

That was a very sobering moment for me. I had crossed a boundary of my own making and had hurt Ted in doing so. I apologized and promised I wouldn't do it again.

"But, Ted," I added, making a meek attempt to defend my actions, "even Dr. Phil says on national TV, 'What the hell were you thinking?'"

That broke the tension, and my apology was accepted.

## ❦ Tongue Twister

We taught our kids a tongue twister Steve learned from his dad, who, coincidentally, *also* loved bathroom humor. We introduced all of Ted and Marshall's dinner guests to it as well. Enunciate clearly as you tell it to your kids, and then ask them to repeat it five times really quickly. Practice a response of abject horror and have fun.

"One smart feller, he felt smart. Two smart fellers, they felt smart."

Simple. Now go ahead and try it out loud without looking at the page.

## ❦ Lost in a Crowd

Whenever we got the chance to visit a theme park or any other large attraction that hundreds of other people had decided to visit, too, we would all wear T-shirts of the same bright color. That way, if either Steve or I lost sight of one of the kids and began to panic, we could simply look down at the shirts we were wearing and start scoping the landscape for a smaller version of the same top. Likewise, if Ted and Marshall found themselves suddenly alone, having had their attention diverted by, say, talking moose heads, they knew immediately what to look for. Iridescent, neon, psychedelic, and jarring. Go for visual impact over fashion; fashion tends to blend in.

## Staying in Sight

Starting when your kids are tots and have earned the privilege of, and developed the confidence for, playing a distance away from you, tell them they must stay where they can see you. Telling them *you* want to be able to see *them* means nothing to them. They figure that since you always seem to know what they've been up to, anyway, you must have eyes in the back of your head, or else they wonder, how are *they* supposed to know what you can or cannot see?

## Deal with it Tomorrow

We always told our boys, "Everything seems harder when you're tired." It reminded us that none of us are at our best when we're bushed, and most decisions are better made after a good night's sleep.

## What to Drink

Before you go anywhere with kids, make sure they are not hungry, are not going to get hungry, are not thirsty, or are not going to get thirsty, and take them to the toilet even if they say they don't need to go. Provide the time and place for a needed nap. Tired, hungry, thirsty kids who have to pee are no fun. The same goes for the accompanying grown-ups, actually. I know, because we saw a lot of cranky kids and adults at theme parks over the years.

Also, starting from when they are too little to know the difference, give your kids water to drink. They do not need the calories or unnecessary sugar (or substitute sweeteners) found in soft drinks and juices. If you wait too long and that's all they've come to know, they will equate liquids with sweetness, and the switch to water will become a battle.

Even now, our sons drink chocolate milk diluted with half an amount of white milk. This is the way the special treat was served to them as kids (to cut down on their sugar intake), and it's the way they still prefer it. They also got apple juice diluted with water and never knew the difference. Young children have no need for soft drinks. When we finally offered them, cola was not on the list. We went for anything that had no caffeine.

## ❦ One of Those Nights

It was Marshall who came up with this idea. I think it stemmed from his desire to include Woody. We had rented a kid flick for Saturday night family viewing.

Normally, all four of us would scrunch in together on the sofa, dim the lights, and spend a couple of hours cozied in with one another. But that wouldn't include Woody, who was not allowed on the furniture. So since the dog wasn't allowed up, it was Marshall's idea we all get down.

And that's what we did. With everyone in their pajamas, we shoved the coffee table aside, spread duvets and blankets, propped everyone's bed pillows up against the sofa, and piled in together. Woody, sensing a new game, immediately picked his way over our tangle of legs and settled himself in at our feet, taking full advantage of all the cushioning—and the stray pieces of popcorn.

This became a new ritual. "One of those nights" is what Marshall dubbed them. "Let's have one of those nights," someone would suggest, and we'd all start clearing furniture and rooting out the blankets.

But don't leap up at the end of the movie. For one thing, you'll miss the outtakes, if there are any. Keep everyone watching all the way through the credits, and you can help your kids learn to scan while reading. A good challenge is for everyone to find how often his or her name appears in the scrolling list. Who knew so many people named Steve worked in show biz?

# CHAPTER 10

## *Osh-ka-ba-ba*

CAMP WABANAKI (OR WAB, FOR SHORT) IS SET LIKE A JEWEL IN THE midst of cottage country three hours north of Toronto. It's just outside Huntsville on the shore of Lake Vernon, one of the many dark water lakes in the district known as Muskoka.

The first year we attended family camp at Wabanaki, Ted had just turned seven, Marshall was four, and I had no hair.

I was doing chemotherapy treatments for stage two breast cancer. "Go ahead," my oncologist urged. "Just two things: don't go in the water, and at the first sign of a fever, get yourself to the closest emergency department."

I didn't develop a fever, and I didn't go in the water—well, not past my ankles, anyway; I did have to get into the canoe. And then I won the couples' canoe challenge: out to the orange marker on the island, then paddling *backward* for the return stretch. Steve helped, of course.

I'd heard about this family camp from a woman with a British accent at the local YMCA, where I had enrolled Marshall in a parents-and-tots playgroup. We struck up a conversation beside the jungle gym as our two boys wormed their way in and out of the red and yellow structure. I knew I liked her when she chortled to me that she thought Marshall had a "dirty" laugh. I'd always just thought of it as contagious.

Anyway, she knew just enough about this program to get me interested, especially the part about not having to cook for five straight days. Steve and I liked what we saw from the promotional brochure, so we signed up and, along with about a dozen other families, moved in to occupy the Y camp (known for its wilderness canoe outtripping program) for the final week of summer.

Each family got its own cabin. Ours was Trailblazer, a rustic structure with little more than narrow wooden bunks, wooden cubbies, and bare light bulbs. Food was forbidden in the cabins since chipmunks could squeeze through the spaces under the doors. The bathrooms, named Harry and Sally, were down the trail and over the hill in separate buildings. None of the cabins had plumbing.

At the opening campfire, we met all the other families. Introductions sounded a lot like what I suspect AA meetings to be like: "Hi, we're the Welches. This is our twelfth year at Wabanaki"—except these were non-recovering family camp junkies. We also met the rest of the staff: a great bunch of energetic young adults who led us through their repertoire of wacky camp songs with increasingly confusing, nonsensical lyrics—*Osh-ka-ba-ba, Hey nonnie, nonnie*—and rapid-fire actions. We sang about sharks—baby sharks and grandpa sharks—and bears and the Princess Pat. Then we all linked pinkies around the fire and swayed side to side to taps: "Day is done, gone the sun."

Morning dip was at 7:15. An enormous dinner bell, mounted on a concrete pedestal, announced each meal, and the kids took turns hanging out around the dining hall door so they'd be picked to pull the rope to ring it. A nighttime snack was served up in the dining hall, too, where Steve and I learned Yahtzee and the kids played Spoons as we noshed on pumpernickel loaves filled with spinach and water chestnut dip, nachos topped with warm stringy cheese and salsa, and hummus and toasty pita triangles—yum!

There was a short paddle to Gull Island—a hump of rounded rock that rose out of Lake Vernon—for a weenie cookout. That was followed by leaps from the rocks into the clear water. We took a separate long paddle in the opposite direction to the ice cream store in Huntsville. Of course, there was talent night: Nate the Great in a fluted, sequined green sheath playing Ariel, the Little Mermaid, with a gaggle of small, shy, and not-so-shy girls singing alongside.

When the tiniest kids hit the ball during the family baseball game, the dads would race in, pick them up, and carry them to first base. Meanwhile, the adult outfielders clumsily missed fly balls, fumbled tosses, and tripped over their own feet so the kids could score runs for their teams.

Marshall won the fishing derby for the biggest fish. Sheila's dad, whom we all called Grandpa Stew (for his last name, Stewart), gave Ted four quarters because he didn't even catch a fish but he kept trying. Sheila had thought to bring her bagpipes to camp (Who takes bagpipes to camp?), and she piped the whole motley crew of us up the hill from the beach the night the cook served turkey dinner with all the fixings. We had a murder mystery night created by counselors who dressed as dwarves or anything else that could be closely represented by what they'd found in the dress-up bag. They came up with scenarios so bizarre they were never solved but they were thoroughly enjoyed. From Monday to Saturday, the days blurred together as we ate, laughed, made gimp bracelets, read novels on the dock, and worked on our new friendships.

Everybody loved that the tanned, fit, can-do counselors were on hand right after breakfast every day to take the kids (and parents, if they wanted) to do crafts and archery and kayaking, and all the other typical camp stuff. They helped anybody who wanted to make tie-dyed T-shirts and hand-dipped candles and rocket launchers; they celebrated if our kids hit even so much as the bale of straw the archery target was attached to, let alone any of the colored rings they were aiming at. And right after lunch, they'd do it all again.

All week, parents were free to wander the island, head into town to shop, or take a nap. The Thursday night wine and cheese party for the adults took place on the beach around a roaring campfire. At some point Roger Woeller, one of the fathers, would take out his guitar, and much, much later the last of us would head to bed.

At the same time, the kids were having their own fun. Mattresses, pillows, and sleeping bags from the cabins were dragged to the rec hall or the dining hall, where counselors camped out with the kids and ate snacks, told stories, and watched movies. (You remember the part about the movies.) Little kids who couldn't stick it out were walked back, hand in hand with a staff member, to wherever their parents were, but *everybody* urged their kids to stay the whole night. We told them it was to practice being a camper, but we were really thinking about having the cabin to ourselves. *Nudge, nudge.*

Our entire family had a wonderful time, so we signed up for the next year. And the year after that.

By then we'd become very familiar with the camp

routines. All of us had mastered the art of getting into a kayak from a dock. We knew the first supper would be make-your-own sandwiches and that the meals would get exponentially better after that. We knew that all kids would consume pretty much their body weight in bacon during their stay, and they would accomplish that by not sitting with their parents for breakfast.

Grandpa Stew would patiently teach kids to fish, day after day, bending the barbs off the hooks to make it easy to release the little sunfish and rock bass and catch the same ones all over again. We knew that Jim Welch (even in his twelfth year as a dad at family camp) would start his war cry halfway down the girls' hill every morning, getting a running start at a cannon ball from the dock for morning dip. Roger and his wife Deb, both veteran campers, gave the rest of us good camp advice like not setting a canoe down on the ground. Deb and Roger had met as teenagers when they were both staff at Wabanaki—many years before. They'd dated, then married, and now they had two little Wab camper girls—which beat out everyone else's "So, how did the two of you meet?" stories.

We knew how to choose the right-size paddle for our canoe treks and were getting pretty good at the J-stroke. Steve and I knew to haul the twin-size mattresses from the bunks and make a queen-size bed on the floor of Trailblazer, our family cabin year after year, by binding the spongy pads together with a fitted mattress cover and a fitted sheet, then topping it off with a cozy duvet.

We also knew how to play out the great family camp gag. At breakfast, partway through the week, within earshot of a new family, Steve would call out to another old-timer, "We're having some problems with the water pressure in Trailblazer's shower. Is yours working okay?"

"Yeah, our shower's fine," someone would answer, "but we ran out of hot water before our Jacuzzi got full."

We knew all these things about our dear Wabanaki, but there was something we'd forgotten to tell Marshall. Steve and I were dressing for the beach when Marshall came through the cabin door after the morning's activity. Flushed with excitement, he turned to face us.

"Did you know kids can come to this camp by themselves? And *not* bring their parents? That's what *I'm* going to do," he added before turning on his heel and rushing out to rejoin his friends.

And that's how we came to have a lifelong love for Camp Wabanaki. Both Ted and Marshall returned the next year as campers for one week. They had the benefit of going with Brian and Kevin, brothers from the same neighborhood back home in Waterloo and of matching ages to Ted and Marshall. This meant that Ted and Brian would forever be assigned the same cabin, as would Marshall and Kevin—kids being divided up by age as they were. Each year, as the registration date approached, all four boys would coordinate their calendars and negotiate with parents for longer and longer camp stays at "camper camp."

Eventually, all of them were spending the entire month of August at Wab without us, paddling the northern waterways being the highlight of the month's experiences. Tales of what transpired at camp would unravel over the course of the year. Marshall's speech for his Grade Five class began "Rain. Rain and thunder. Rain, thunder, and lightning. That's when the little kid in the middle of the tent threw up."

Kevin was in that tent, too. You might think that type of thing would dampen a kid's appetite to do it all over again, but it didn't. All four boys continued through the camper years, completing the leader-in-training course and finishing with the counselor-in-training summer. All were hired as Wab counselors themselves. Beyond that, they took positions as waterfront director, leader-in-training trainer, out-tripping leader, and staff leader.

At the end of each summer, Steve and I would meet up with our sons in the camp parking lot, their duffel bags filled with laundry. An afternoon at the Laundromat later, we would check into a local motel, grab a bite, and hear some of what had gone on through the summer. The next morning, we'd check back into Wab. Steve and I would head down to make ourselves cozy in Trail-blazer and wait for the arrival of friends, old and new, for that year's session of family camp. Ted and Marshall no longer slept with us; they had their places in staff cabins, but we'd meet up later that night. When introductions were being made around the opening campfire, one of us would stand up and say, "We're the Parsons-Jefferies . . ."

We made it as far as tying the Welches. ". . . and this is our twelfth year at family camp."

## ❦Learning the Hard Way

Never, ever, from a standing position, put one foot on a dock and the other foot inside a floating kayak.

## ❦The Things You Never Knew

There were many serendipitous discoveries that came from sharing a cabin with our sons. We discovered that Marshall talked in his sleep. A lot. We also found that he'd sit bolt upright in his bunk nightly, roused by some dreamtime stimulus, and reach for something, midair, near the end of his bed.

"Food," he explained. "It always makes me sad when it's not really there."

## ❦Camp Culture

Even knowing how wasteful this sounds, I still give this seasoned advice to all camper parents: on your children's return home, just throw the socks out. If any socks come back at all. Also, be reassured—the condition of your camper child's feet has a name: permadirt. It generally sloughs off by about Halloween.

Camp culture provided a great platform from which to deal with any strong language Ted and Marshall might be exposed to—for instance, if their parents had a mental lapse and brought home a movie like *True Lies* for "one of those nights." Expletives were quickly followed by a stern pronouncement: "*Those* aren't Wab words!"

## 𝕎 You Have to *Tell* Them

We forget sometimes that our kids perceive things very differently than we do because they don't have all the info, and so their behavior may confuse us. I remember sitting with a very good friend after lunch one summer day. Ted was barely two. We were having chilled watermelon for dessert. Despite the fact he wore a soft plastic bib with a trough for catching the bright red juice that poured from his chin, most of it was running under the collar and soaking his T-shirt.

"I wonder when Ted will figure out that when you eat watermelon, you're supposed to suck the juice in as you take a bite, like this." I posed my query to my longtime friend as I inhaled air loudly through my teeth.

Ted tipped his head slightly to the left and gave me an odd look. Then, with his next bite, he sucked and slurped every drop of melon juice into his mouth and swallowed with a satisfied gulp. "Is there anything else you've forgotten to tell me?" he seemed to say.

Another eye-opening experience involved Marshall. We had all awakened early on a winter's morning. Breakfast was finished, and snow pants, mittens, and hats were at the ready. We were on our way for a family ski day at a resort three hours north. Both Ted and Marshall had gone to bed excited the night before, with lots of chatter about what this day would hold. Ted at age seven had already tried skiing, taking a few lessons and progressing quickly from the bunny hill to the chairlift. The first run he took with his dad ended with a stern lecture at the bottom of a relatively steep grade.

"Ted!" Steve snapped as he finally caught up with our elder son, who had taken off from the top of the hill and whooshed straight down to the flats where people were joining the lift line. "You have to *turn*! That's what the lessons were for—to teach you to ski in control. The instructor said you knew how to do it!"

"I *do* know," Ted insisted, "but I don't want to—it slows me down."

So Ted the thrill seeker was eager to get going, and Marshall seemed to share the enthusiasm—right until he saw our sports equipment being loaded into the rooftop carrier.

"I've changed my mind," Marshall said. "I'm not going."

Given that not going was not an option, I explained to Marshall that this was a family day and we were *all* going. There was a lesson already booked for him, reservations had been made for his ski rental, everyone was dressed, the car was packed, and we were going.

"Okay," he relented. "I'll go, but I'm not skiing."

Once there, Steve and I swung our skis and poles onto our shoulders and, despite his protestations, got Marshall to at least follow us from the parking lot to take a look at what was waiting for him in the rental shop.

A friendly young man leaned over the counter and peered down at our little son. "I have just the thing for you," he said, smiling, and then disappeared among the racks of equipment. Reemerging, he set a pair of miniature skis on the counter and began to adjust the bindings.

"What are those?" Marshall asked.

"They're your skis," I explained, wondering what he thought they were.

"Oh." There was long pause as his thinking shifted. "I think I'd like to ski after all."

It wasn't until we were out on the slopes that Steve figured it out. No one had thought to tell Marshall he'd be getting a set of skis proportionate to his size—reaching in height somewhere between his nose and his forehead. He had taken one look at the monstrously long sets we had loaded into the van—nearly twice his height—and had decided that strapping himself to something like that meant certain death.

## ᴡ Conservation of Size

Sometimes the way kids see things is just plain funny, precisely because they are unrestrained by the parameters of reality. Thus, their world is joyfully open to occurrences of pure magic.

There is an opening sequence in the animated movie *Rescuers Down Under*. As viewers, we are propelled rapidly forward as if piloting a crop-dusting, low-flying airplane over a meadow. Distance is eaten up at a dizzying speed. Marshall had just learned to ride a two-wheeler with training wheels when he saw that clip. "Hey," he cried out, "that's just like me riding my bike!"

Then there is the case of "shrinking tunnels." I expect you've seen them, although you may to this day be unaware of their workings. They are lengthy concrete structures—tunnels—that extend from a highway or freeway at an angle.

"What are you talking about?" I asked Ted and Marshall as they whooped and hooted in the backseat on a trip into Toronto, "What shrinking tunnels?"

"Watch," they explained, "See that red car going in this end? Wait till you see what size it is when it comes out!"

Tiny. In developmental psychology, the understanding that objects do not actually morph in dimension as they approach or recede is known as conservation of size.

## ▼ A Teacher's Wisdom

When Ted and Marshall headed off to camp as counselors, I sent with them some wisdom I'd inherited from Pauline Hamel. An experienced teacher, she taught Grade One down the hall from where I taught. I wanted to *be* Pauline Hamel. She was poised and calm and elegant and confident and, well, I wasn't any of those. Also, her kids always behaved in the hallways.

Because small kids have small bladders, all the primary grade teachers at our school had a scheduled washroom break every morning and afternoon. My class followed Pauline's.

Now, I figure the students I had in my first year of teaching learned in spite of me rather than because of me. My only real accomplishment was figuring out how to take twenty-five children to the bathroom and back without having the entire school come down on our heads. And that's where Pauline came in.

One day my class waited in the wings as Pauline's group was forming nice tidy lines outside the washroom doors: one for girls, one for boys. They were quietly waiting for the stragglers who were still in there doing their business. Someone in the line made a loud, somewhat rude comment about what was probably going on in the bathroom. Pauline was at that kid's side (okay, let's be honest—it was a boy) in a flash. Her normally pleasant, soft expression had hardened somewhat, morphing from mildly disappointed to downright stern. Bending over, she put her lips to the boy's ear and whispered. All the other kids stood like pillars of salt.

I watched as the misbehaving child's head nodded, then nodded again. Then, with everything under complete control, Pauline's class exited, with precision, to the right, leaving the space open for my students to take over.

"What did you *say* to that kid?" I asked her later, hoping for some guidance.

"It doesn't so much matter *what* you say," she explained. "The thing is to make it private. I just told him that what he said was not acceptable and I didn't ever want him talking that way again—and I asked him if he understood."

I can tell you more than that. From the looks on all the *other* kids' faces, *none* of them wanted to have their beloved Miss Hamel come and bend over to whisper in their ears like that, *ever*! They didn't have a clue what she had said, nor did they want to find out.

"You see," Pauline continued, "I could have just stood there and given the same lecture, out loud, from the front of the group, but that way it's like *everybody* is in a *little bit* of trouble, and the kid who acted up gets the same watered-down dose of medicine the other twenty kids do. This way, the kid who misbehaved *knows* who he or she is, and so does everyone else."

"You can use that advice with your campers," I mentored Ted and Marshall. "Discipline privately."

That's good advice for us all. And remember the rest

of what Miss Hamel told me: let *everybody* hear you compliment kids on a job well-done."

So, when you're within earshot of your kids, let them overhear you tell Grandma or the neighbor about something kind, polite, or thoughtful they did that day. And don't shame them publicly.

## Let Your Children Go

Our job is to equip our children with the skills and experiences they need to become capable, responsible, independent young adults no matter how often we have to weep, cry "Ow!", or clutch our hearts as they walk out the door. Many of us would choose to keep our kids with us all summer—all year—forever. It's important to remember: this is not about *you* and what you want, it's about *them*. You've put in many parenting hours teaching them to not be selfish. This is the time to remind yourself of the same lesson.

Kids need to learn how to make good choices away from our constant scrutiny. A good camp is an ideal starting place. Begin with sleepovers with the friend next door, then pack more stuff and send them off for a weekend with dear Aunt Kate, but let your kids go. And don't just let your kids go to *camp*; learn how to let them go out into the big, big world to see it from their perspective. If we've done a good job as parents, it's where they're going to want to live.

## ❦ Boys Do, Girls Talk

I remember hearing a great description of one of the differences between boys and girls.

A boy knows he's found a friend when the new boy wants to *do* stuff with him: shoot hoops, build a raft, dam a creek. A girl knows she's found a friend when the new girl will *talk* to her: tell her secrets and confide in her.

So imagine the confusion when, at a later age and stage, boys and girls get interested in each other. A boy thinks a girl doesn't like him because she never wants to *do* anything. All she wants to do is sit around and *talk*—like about feelings and stuff! A girl thinks a boy doesn't like her because all he ever wants is to go out and *do* stuff, and he never talks to her about anything!

To this day, Ted and Marshall can spend an entire weekend with Brian and Kevin—a rare and precious occurrence—and when I question them later, I will know next to *nothing* about what their friends are up to. "But didn't you ask them?" I press for more information. "What did you *talk* about all weekend?!"

"I don't know," they can now say in nearly perfect unison. "We just hung out and did stuff."

So if you have boys, get out there and *do* stuff with them. Maybe you'll catch them off guard, and they'll start talking.

## ❦ The Male of the Species

To help understand what's going on inside your sons' little heads, read anthologies of *Calvin and Hobbs* comic strips. You will gain insight into how boys—and, for that matter, men—see the world. Your challenge is to embrace a new view that is at once delightful, refreshing, and weirdly perplexing.

# CHAPTER 11

## *Home Sweet Home, Sweet Home, Sweet Home*

OUR FAMILY HAS LIVED IN LOTS OF DIFFERENT PLACES. WE MOVED from one continent to another when Ted was three weeks old, then from one city to another when he was one. We moved again when he was eleven, twelve, thirteen, and sixteen. Of course, Marshall came, too. For the most part, we moved to pursue dreams of better schooling and the chance to live our lives closer to nature. In equal parts, our dreams have come true.

I remember telling a cousin of Steve's we were going to sell our house. She was shocked. "Why would you move?" she asked. "That's your *home!*"

We know we're the odd ones out, but that thinking escapes us; *everywhere* we've lived has been our home. The trick has been to move in completely, right off the bat. Boxes get unpacked, walls get painted, and art gets hung, so we have our familiar things in familiar places— so we *feel* at home. The only challenge has been to look for and capitalize on the best features of each house, neighborhood, and community and accommodate the inherent limitations. As we reminisce, we refer to our many homes by their location: Gipps Street, Mill Street, Knightsbridge, Lakewood, Elgin Street, Parklane.

Our big house in Waterloo where both boys started school was Ted's third home. That was "Knightsbridge," named after the cul-de-sac we lived on. We took advantage of the amenities available in that community: gymnastics classes, Cub Scouts, piano lessons, church, soccer, T-ball, and drive-through car washes.

That house backed onto the boys' schoolyard, and there was a baseball diamond directly behind our gate. We took turns taking Ted out there to practice hitting before he signed up with the rest of the kids for the T-ball league. On game day, his first hit connected with a resounding whack.

"Run, Ted!" his coach cheered. "Run!"

Ted looked confused for a moment and then took off pell-mell—to the pitcher's mound. We should have practiced running bases, too.

Just like something you might see in the movies, when Woody heard the school bell ring at the end of the day, he used to head out to that playing field to wait for Marshall and Ted. We stopped letting him outside the gate, though, after the time he didn't reappear with his boys on the back step. We looked everywhere. We hopped into the van and drove around the neighborhood, calling his name. Returning to the house, I noticed the message light flashing on our phone. A very nice woman had called to assure us her daughter had found a lost yellow dog at her schoolyard. Our phone number was on his collar's tag.

The girl had just looped her fingers through his collar, and Woody had happily followed her all the way home— right past the open gate to our yard.

Our Knightsbridge house had a bright, spacious family room that opened onto the kitchen. The boys were allowed to spread out their toys there and create playscapes that could stay put for a few days: little log cabins, castle siege scenes, towers of plastic tubing for marble races. Until they needed to be dusted or vacuumed underneath, they could remain in place, giving Ted and Marshall the chance to expand on their fantasies and challenges.

On the tiled floor of the kitchen nook stood a child's paint easel, fully stocked with plain newsprint paper and pots filled with multihued tempera paints, a brush stuck in each pot to avoid cross-color contamination. A smock hung from the top corner. Because of the lesson I learned from Ted decorating our powder room, I made it very clear, right from the learning stages, how to use it neatly. "These are the edges of the paper," I showed Ted and Marshall, tracing my finger around the perimeter of a page. "Keep the paint inside this line." Naturally, the boys weren't completely successful keeping the medium off the edges of the easel, but they did seem to get my point about staying away from the adjacent wall.

There was space in the family room for a tall, four-drawer cabinet against the wall beside the play table. Each drawer held things from a different category. Paper and popsicle sticks, pipe cleaners, and glitter could be found among the play dough and felt squares in the craft drawer. Another held buckets of Lego blocks and Playmobil characters. A third was filled with cars, trucks, trains, and planes. But the fun always began with a foray into the dress-up drawer. It held a treasure trove of vests and hats and helmets and shields and a homemade cape given to Ted as a birthday gift—maybe his best present *ever*. There were pirate things and cowboy things, and a lot of guns, swords, bows and arrows, and targets.

On some days Ted and Marshall pulled the cushions off our two sofas or took an old sheet to drape over the dining room table. They created forts and castles that needed to be filled with snack-like provisions and defended from invaders. On other days they went out to the backyard and made use of the play center, with its sandbox and elevated fort. At still other times they took the old sheet, draped it like a theater curtain along the crosspiece of the swing set, and put on magic shows and acts of daring and courage (some of which included a dog) for their invited guests: Steve and me.

In the backyard, Steve, Ted, and Marshall cut a small garden in the shape of Mickey Mouse's head. Steve helped the boys plant three different varieties of tomatoes for them to water and tend during the summer, then harvest when the crop was ready.

On a summer afternoon, we would pitch their small tent on the flat grass close to the back door. With snacks, flashlights, pillows, sleeping bags, and a very long extension cord for the little TV with the VCR, the kids would camp out with Woody for the night. Or some part of the night.

We loved that house and the friends we made living there, but for a couple of years in a row, the teachers went on strike. As a result, the kids were locked out of their school with no materials to continue their studies. It wasn't a model for conflict resolution Steve and I wanted our boys adopting, so we decided to go looking for a school board where the quality of teaching was good and relations were a little more stable.

We bought an exquisite log home just steps from the shore of Georgian Bay in Ontario's ski country. It reminded us of *Little House on the Prairie,* since you could stand in one spot inside the tiny house and see pretty much everything we owned. We knew it was too small when we bought it, but it had a rustic elegance we fell in love with. We decided to try living minimally for one year, at which point we could decide whether building an addition seemed the right thing to do. So we had a big garage sale and sold a lot of furniture. Then we bought some other furniture and moved into the tiny cabin, making optimal use of every space.

Marshall got the bigger of the boys' bedrooms, and rightly so, having had the smaller one in our last home. We made room alongside his bunks for a couple of zebra-striped floor mats and a low bookcase to house all the books and bins of construction toys.

Ted and Marshall's friends all came to visit whenever they could, but Brian and Kevin were the first guests. They pulled the trundle out from under the lower bunk and made space for everyone to sleep.

Both boys had their own desks. Ted had the little TV and the video game console on the corner of his desk. That way, toy time and screen time were equally divided between the two bedrooms. There was no TV reception in that cabin, and rather than having anything installed, we decided to live the year without watching the shows we thought we *couldn't* live without. And all of us did just fine. Actually, I cheated the night of the Oscars; I plugged in the little TV set we used in the van and dragged a weak signal into the cabin with the rabbit ears.

The power frequently went out in the area for a few

hours at a time. Whenever that happened at night, we made it a custom to play charades or "Who Am I?" by candlelight. The art materials were still in a drawer in the dining room, and our sons experimented with sketching and watercolor, both indoors and out. Harry Potter books were consumed as they were released. Together, Ted and Marshall built a rope swing in the tree behind the cabin.

The challenge involved a tall stepladder. As they headed out to play Tarzan from heights that would make the blood run backward in my veins, I would repeat the mother's mantra that Steve had provided me for situations like this: Just don't look.

The boys (supervised and wearing PFDs) also plied the shore of the chilly bay just beyond our property line in an inflatable rubber raft. They explored new territory by crawling through the drainage pipe that ran beneath the highway at the end of our road, but essentially our sons were landlocked. We had the bay on one side and a busy highway on the other, giving them not enough freedom to do the things they were ready to do, like bike to the video store without adult accompaniment. And the cabin had little brown bats—*lots* of little brown bats. They're a protected species, the exterminator explained.

After living there for just eleven months, we put that house on the market (and included the appliances). It sold in one day. Because we couldn't find a house in the town nearby where we *wanted* to live, we rented a condo at the base of the local ski resort. Our unit overlooked the first tee of the development's golf course. Ted and Marshall shared a bedroom now, with the bunks separated into matching twin beds. That left the den on the main floor for their play space and their TV watching.

Brian and Kevin were the first to visit.

We stayed in the condo for just over half a year. Ted and Marshall spent much of that winter perfecting their snowboarding skills. They took a walkie-talkie with them to the slopes, since cell phones were not so popular yet, and they loved to buzz us at the condo and urge us out onto balcony.

"See those two kids standing under the chairlift waving like crazy?" they'd ask. "That's us!" Something about that struck them as funny—like maybe Steve and I would figure out the only way they got there was down an incredibly steep run, and the only way to the bottom was more of the same terrain.

During the warm months, Woody and I headed out very early in the morning to the rough and the ravines of the golf course. We found lots of golf balls.

So at age twelve, Ted launched his first career as owner and manager of a business he called White Spot. He subcontracted work to Marshall at an hourly rate, and together they cleaned those golf balls and set up a table with a cash box, a battery-powered boom box, a cooler full of drinks, a shade umbrella, and a walkie-talkie to call for a ride home. They staked out a place on public land, just far enough along the course for golfers who had lost *their* golf balls to be in need of some more.

Steve coached the boys in marketing and sales strategies. The training came in useful the day a potential customer complained, from his perch on his golf cart, that their prices were too high, that he could buy golf balls in town for much less.

"Well, sir," was the response he got, "you are welcome to do that—drive into town for more golf balls, but if you prefer the convenience of *our* location, *these* are our prices."

Ted cleared $800 in sales that summer and bought himself a drum kit.

Still we continued our real estate quest. Eventually, we found a home in Thornbury—the little town we'd wished for: a sprawling 1970s ranch-style bungalow.

As the movers were unloading the last of our possessions into our new place, Marshall turned to me and asked, "Do you think we could stay here for a while?"

And we did. This home had space in the basement (or "lower level," as we came to refer to it) for Ted and Marshall to have their own bedrooms away from their parents. It had extra bedrooms for sleepover guests, too, so, we bought a bunch more furniture at garage sales and filled those rooms up with vintage pieces refreshed with a coat of paint. As with our other moves, Brian and Kevin were the first to be invited.

We had made arrangements for a local handyman to come as soon as he could and do some much-needed renovations. Most important, Marshall's bedroom didn't have a window in it, so technically it couldn't really be *called* a bedroom. Nor did it have a door. These were things that needed to be rectified quickly. Since Brian and Kevin arrived days before the handyman, the boys simply hung an old sheet over the door frame for privacy and spent a lot of that first weekend eating snacks and laughing in the dark.

The house was wonderfully laid out for the ages and the stage we were all at. There was a rec room downstairs with lots of square footage for guitars and drums, so Ted and Marshall formed their first band and took up songwriting with Kimble, a talented young friend.

We had space in the rec room, too, for a used pool table we were given as a gift. On Saturday nights, we'd have tournaments and eat fondue at the built-in bar. By that time, our dear aging Woody didn't want to go up and down the stairs, so he stayed on the main level and missed out on those billiard challenges. But he *was* paying attention.

Just as Steve was about to make an important shot one evening, there was a horrendous, continuous clatter and clanging and pinging nearby. We all hustled to see what in Sam Hill's name had happened to our house.

There, at the top of the stairs, staring down at the four of us, stood Woody. At the bottom of the stairs, his metal dish was spinning its last few revolutions across the carpet at our feet.

It was 6:27 PM. Woody ate at 6:00—on the dot. Put out by our seemingly neglectful disregard for the hour, he had finally walked to the laundry room, picked his dish up in his teeth, carried it through the kitchen, and, leaning forward on the top step, let it go so it would drop the thirteen stairs to the basement to get our attention. He made his point. We loved that dog.

The backyard wasn't very big, but there was enough space in it for a trampoline, so we bought one, used, from a friend. Ted and Marshall had been instructed at gymnastics classes in the skills they needed to enjoy it. Everyone who used it was directed to abide by our three rules: no bleeding, no broken bones, and have fun.

Actually, there was a fourth rule. Our sons had begun taking a boom box outside with them so they could play tunes as they bounced. "Keep it down, please," I told them. Our new neighbors, Harvey and Jean, enjoyed a lot of time on the patio in their backyard. Our trampoline was fully in their view.

I thought there was going to be trouble the day Harvey rose from his chair on that patio and came across their yard into ours. I was hanging laundry on the line. The boys were bouncing to tunes. Quiet tunes, I thought.

Harvey approached me and moved into what I would call my personal space. He stood, arms akimbo, and said gruffly, "I don't know where you got that trampoline, but I think you need to go back and find the people you bought it from and give them a *lot* more money. I've never seen two boys have so much fun."

He was a nice man, that Harvey.

A stretch of empty lots spanned the bottom of our street, and in the middle of one of them stood a magnificent weeping willow tree. Something about it sparked a dream in Marshall, and with Steve's help and multiple trips to the lumber center, Marshall built a sturdy spacious tree fort in the crook of the largest spreading branches.

Marshall loved that leafy retreat. He'd come home from school, grab a snack and a novel, and climb the wooden stairs to the platform. It was perfect except for one thing.

We had neglected to consult the owner of that property. We didn't know who he was, but *he* found out who *we* were and told Marshall the fort had to come down. We offered to sign a waiver releasing him from any liability, but in the end, the answer was still no.

So we apologized to the man for not asking permission, and then Ted and Marshall used that lumber to build skateboarding ramps on our driveway. When the snow fell, and *with* the permission of a very senior woman who owned the white frame house with the big long hill at the *other* end of our street, they lugged all manner of boards and plywood sheeting into her yard and built snowboard and toboggan jumps.

Alongside our driveway, they built a warren of igloos and, taking more snack-like provisions with them, spent lots of hours with friends, adding décor statements and furnishings like benches, beds, and footstools made from the snow that just kept falling.

In May and June, before the school year ended, they would head to the harbor on their bikes, joining other preteens and teens jumping from the pier into the clear, cold water of Georgian Bay. In those months, Marshall also pursued his interest in soccer. He was a good goal-keeper, getting as tall as he was. He could spread his limbs and fill up a big portion of the net, blocking the opposing team's shots on goal.

Marshall enjoyed soccer, but he loved Camp Wabanaki. Since leaving for camp meant abandoning his team as they neared playoffs, Marshall made the tough choice and dropped out of the sport.

Ted had played baseball for a number of seasons. Deciding his summers at Wabanaki with Marshall, Brian, and Kevin were more important, he too stopped playing—but not before he mastered running the bases in order.

Marshall took a certified babysitter's course at the local library and made some extra money on weekends. Ted worked for a while washing dishes at a local pub. It was an exciting promotion for him when they assigned him to making sandwiches.

Our sons were growing up—as in tall. The home where we had spent the past four years no longer fit us. The ceilings in the center hallway on the lower level were six feet two inches high. At sixteen and fourteen, both Ted and Marshall were nearing that mark. Their growth showed no signs of slowing, so we moved.

## ❦ Fostering Inspiration

"I'm bored." Those are two of the most exciting words I could hear, as a mom; it meant that before long, something inspired was going to happen at our house.

When I worked as a teacher, I couldn't help but notice a difference between the city kids I taught in my first five years and the rural kids I worked with after that. Ever so generally speaking, the country kids were more grounded and seemed to display a more solid sense of self-worth. When I thought about it, I recognized that for many of them, their place in the family was meaningful and purposeful. If *they* didn't collect the eggs, feed the cattle, hoe the garden, or pick the beans, *someone* had to.

On the other hand, many of my city students' weekly calendars were jammed full of activities. They were constantly being shuttled from lessons to classes to practices to events: piano, soccer, ballet, Cub Scouts, hockey, choir—the lists went on and on. But what if they just didn't show up? Was their absence of any real-life consequence? And when did they have time to lie on their backs and find shapes in the clouds?

Informed by those observations and limited by the reality that neither Steve nor I would be bringing home any chickens or cows to create truly meaningful chores for our children, we decided to at least limit the number of scheduled activities our kids would participate in during any given season to two. They might not have eggs to collect, but they *would* be given time to find chicken shapes in the clouds. And help with household chores.

The trick was, as Miss Manners would coach, to discourage boredom with the following tactic: faced with the nagging question "What can I do?" suggest a limited number of activities that could fill the empty space in your child's day. Choose something like creating a diorama using Plasticene and a shoe box; going outside with a prism, a magnet, and a magnifying glass; or building something with marshmallows and plastic straws. Should they balk at your ideas, suggest that the time be profitably spent cleaning their bedrooms.

After making your best offer of ideas, I would suggest you keep quiet. First, your kids will come to the understanding that you are not going to solve their boredom issues. Second, it's only within the "white" space you create with silence that inspiration will be visited upon them.

## ᐯ Our Children's Job

Our children's job is to play.

No, it's not. Our children's job is to grow. Throughout childhood, they achieve much of what they learn and master—major developmental hurdles such as motor function, language, and social skills—*through* play. They discover pathways to innovation and problem solving. They get to explore interdependence and independence.

Our job as parents (as Steve has so faithfully reminded me) is to *help* our children grow. Unfortunately, our job is *not* to get our kids to cooperate, which I think would make life much easier, less dangerous, and far more predictable. What our kids need from us is oodles and oodles of unstructured playtime away from electronic things and electrical sockets. Kids need to be in relationship with nature and friends (face-to-face); they need us to support their varied (and possibly fleeting) interests, and we need to willingly provide appropriate supervision—and possibly PFDs.

## Know the Rules

Be very clear in your own mind what the rules should be for any given activity. Keep the list short and consistent, because if *you* can't remember what the rules are, how will your kids? Remember, it's always a gift to your children as well as to yourself if the last of your rules is "have fun."

## Who Am I?

The game "Who Am I?" is easy to play and teaches kids questioning skills. Pin a piece of paper to the back of one player's shirt. On it someone will have printed the name of a person, an animal, or a character the player knows or knows of—anyone from a friend on the street to President Obama. Don't let the player see what is written on it, and don't tell him or her. The player then moves about the room, turning his or her back to the rest of the players so they can read the name.

The player then begins asking questions of the others to determine the answer to the puzzle "Who am I?" The trick is that questions can only be answered yes or no (with the smallest bits of fudging to help your kids be successful). Thus, the player can't ask, "How old am I?" but instead needs to figure out how to determine the age of the character some other way, such as "Am I older than ten?"

Adults can demonstrate a few turns to help the kids get the drift.

"Am I alive?" An answer of no to that question doesn't mean you're dead. "Am I real?" or "Am I a fictional character?" might provide a clue. "Have I met this person?" and "Am I male?" are also good questions. (You can't ask "Am I male or female?" because that requires an answer other than yes or no.)

Am I famous? Do I sing? Do I live in this town? Am I human? Hmm.

## ᵂ What's That You Say?

It's not as though Ted *couldn't* have known where to run after he hit that ball; we used to pile in together on the sofa and watch televised baseball as a family, but there's a lot to explain and a lot to decipher, and sometimes we're not exactly clear with our kids. I know that from the day Marshall said he wanted the Toronto Blue Jays to beat the New York Hankies.

## ᵂ Keep Toy Choice Interesting

On a fairly regular basis, change the play experience for your kids. Put away toys that have temporarily lost their appeal (we used the bare shelves of our linen closet for that) and replace them with things they haven't seen for quite a while. Mix up the combinations, too. Perhaps you can add to their fun by taking advantage of local toy lending "libraries," such as a YMCA, or swap with a friend for a month.

## ᵂ Creative Playing

Friends we knew used to insist their children play with just one toy at a time. That item had to be put away before a next toy was taken from the toy chest. That can be unnecessarily limiting; by allowing your children to incorporate several elements or playthings, you foster creativity, which is simply the ability to connect previously unconnected ideas.

## ❦Fighting over a Toy

How is it that a toy can sit idle on a shelf for days or weeks, but the moment one kid picks it up, the *other* wants it—immediately?

We told our sons they were to use their words to solve their difficulties, hitting not being allowed between *any* family members, but it doesn't take a parent long to understand that kids might indeed use words, but they may not be the helpful kind. So here are the words we taught them to say; we call this Negotiating 101.

First, the one who wants it has to say, "I want a turn with that toy." *"Please"* would be a nice addition, but it's not required, given that integrating negotiating skills *and* manners sounds like a third-tier course.

Next, the one who has the toy gets to respond, "You can have it in x minutes." Now, this has to be a number much smaller than 10,000, which is what they *want* to say. Suggest something under ten. Kids who've repeatedly had ten-minute warnings given at playdates have a fairly good sense of how long that is.

It is then the responsibility of the one who wants the toy to register a formal request for a time check with the nearby adult, who, in turn, gives interval warnings to the one who has the toy. Don't fudge on the time check. This is another opportunity for your kids to practice delayed gratification. But don't be surprised if, in ten minutes, they've forgotten what it was they wanted so badly and have moved on to something else.

You may think this sounds complicated, but it is way easier than listening to ten minutes of whining or bickering.

## 🌱 Artwork

Having an easel in the house can generate a lot of large-scale art.

A neighbor had her own way of dealing with the volume of paintings and drawings her daughter generated. She'd throw them out when the girl wasn't around. If, by chance, her daughter spotted one of her creations in the kitchen bin at the end of the island, my friend would simply act surprised and exclaim (as she did a dumpster dive and began uncrinkling the masterpiece), "Now, how did that get in there? The wind must have blown it off the counter!"

I'm not a good liar. I find it far too hard to remember what embellishments I might have told to what person and when or why, and then the whole thing gets too complicated, so generally speaking, I just tell the truth to make my life *easier*. My choice, when it came to dealing with the overabundance of artwork at our house, was to just explain to our boys that we couldn't keep it all and let them choose something of which they were especially proud to hang on the fridge or in a frame in their bedroom. Over time, they'd make new selections and part with the old. Selected treasures went into a scrapbook.

## 𝘞 Display Accomplishments

Print photos of your kids at their proudest moments: the jump from the high diving board, the first bicycle run down the driveway without training wheels, or the piano recital. Mount them in a collection of small picture frames to display on dresser tops and bedside tables. Hang a bulletin board in their room for certificates and ribbons. Display their trophies. If they ever have a low moment and doubt their abilities, point out the evidence of all they've accomplished in their best moments.

## 𝘞 Screaming in the Car Wash

Despite the fact that moving so often meant we had to leave behind many friendships and attachments, there were certain traditions we kept wherever we went, and not all of them made sense to other families. We screamed our heads off inside automatic car washes. I don't why—it was just a kind of primal therapy as the lather coated the windows and torrents of water crashed down on us. We'd all end up laughing and trying to appear normal by the time jets of air were clearing the windshield and the motorized track threatened to propel us back out into society.

The more harried the week, the cleaner the car.

## 🌱Leaving Our Mark

We signed every house we left. Somewhere, on a crawl space rafter, inside an attic access, or just above the baseboard in someone's closet, you will find our names and the span of years we called that place home.

# CHAPTER 12

## *So Where Are You From, Exactly?*

THE FINAL MOVE WE MADE AS A FAMILY—THE LAST PLACE WE would all live together under one roof—was the town nearby that boasted the region's high school and a river for kayaking.

The house we bought had high ceilings but not as much space, so before we moved, we chose the pieces of furniture we wanted to keep, put the rest on the driveway, and held another garage sale. The house was smaller but the yard was bigger. There was lots of room for the trampoline, and our property backed onto a glorious municipal park, where there was an old growth forest to explore just beyond our fence line. Our first year there, we gave Marshall a metal outdoor fireplace as his year-end gift, which seemed like an odd present for a kid who had just reached his teens, but on nice evenings we would all sit out by the fire. Marshall and Ted would bring out their guitars and we'd watch the stars and hope for fireflies.

The band the boys had joined expanded, and, with pooled finances, the kids paid a local sound technician to record a CD of their original music. They got to perform at some local teen events and occasionally contributed their music to the worship service at church.

They continued to play outdoors: basketball, mountain biking, and snowboarding. They lugged the lumber salvaged from the tree fort into the park and set up rails and jumps on the slopes to challenge their snowboarding skills. Marshall picked up an interest in photography and videography. The two boys would return from their adventures and call me over to the computer monitor to watch what they had captured on camera. I learned it is best to discover what your kids have done and survived than to ask what their plan is as they're heading out the door.

It was at this house our sons transitioned from the phase in which they were loath to shower to the one in which Steve and I were loath to pay the water bill. Both Ted and Marshall had taken what seemed to me a startling interest in personal hygiene. Perhaps I should have anticipated it.

At an annual checkup with our trusted pediatrician, Dr. Munk, ever so many years before, Steve had asked if there were any tricks to getting a kid to stop picking his nose.

"Dating usually cures it," he responded.

So too there seemed to be a link between dating and showering. Arguments arose between the boys about who got to bathe first and when it was time to get out.

Steve's solution was to create and post a computer-generated schedule for who got to shower first on which mornings. Mine was to hang a waterproof clock on a rope from the showerhead.

During our years in that home, both sons had the tremendous good fortune to travel to Europe with school groups—Ted with the orchestra, Marshall with his history teachers—proving to me that times had truly changed. I too had traveled with my school friends on a class trip—it was in celebration of our elementary school graduation. We went to Niagara Falls on a bus. For the day. I'm pretty sure we took our own lunch.

Ted and Marshall started spending more time on the golf course, often with Steve. I gave golf a try, but it escaped me how it came to be called a game. I know a game when I see one, and it's supposed to be fun, *not* make me feel like cursing.

The boys dated very nice girls. There isn't a lot more I can add to that, since boys don't talk. There was an apparent code of silence between our sons, which I discovered when I once asked Ted whether he thought Marshall's interest in a particular girl was romantic.

"I wouldn't have a clue," he answered. That was Ted's polite way of telling me he *wouldn't* tell me, even if he did know. Which he most likely did.

Steve and I spent our summers without the boys as they took jobs at camp; then, having spent so many summers regulated by the same precise timetable, they moved on to become greens keepers at golf resorts.

It was from this home that Ted left for university. Lambie went with him. I suggested that she be blind-folded or put someplace—like maybe a drawer or a closet —where she wouldn't have to witness everything that might go on in a dorm room, since she was so precious and all.

Marshall, in anticipation of his best friend leaving home and being smart enough to predict that this could mean spending much more time with his parents, fostered close friendships with classmates as Ted's departure drew nearer.

A group of them formed a new band. They practiced in our basement on the cast-off purple shag carpet and performed at the high school's talent contests and at local venues.

Marshall repurposed the old lumber, added more boards, and constructed a mountain biking challenge in the woods. A continuous, snaking pathway of narrowing and broadening boards and ramps rose and dipped over fallen trees. The first major snowfall found him with his new pal farther back in the forest, piling snow into an enormous mound to form a quinzee—an igloo-like shelter. He and his friend positioned the doorway to their structure so it faced the steep slope of the hill that rose to the bluff above. Then having also created a hard-packed slide along its descent, they would climb the hill and launch themselves down the icy chute to arrive, feet first, inside the snow fort.

Having earned a snowboard instructor's certificate, Marshall began working weekends at the ski hill, employed to catch-and-release youngsters as they learned to snowboard. The learning curve for this involved so much falling down that Marshall likened it to being in a three-day car wreck.

Then Marshall also left for university. He couldn't take Spy, the stuffed black and white kitten he'd cuddled as a little boy. At about the age of four, he'd left Spy on the subway during a family trip to Toronto. It didn't faze Marshall. "I'll just get another one," he told us. Instead, Marshall headed off to university in the company of his new best buddy, Travis, who, I suppose, was Spy's replacement.

Steve and I spent another year together in that home by the forest. It was very quiet, and we came to realize that neither Ted nor Marshall would be returning to that small town. They had bigger dreams to pursue. With them gone, the allure of the town wore off for us, too. So we had another garage sale. We sold some furniture and bought some other furniture, left the appliances, and moved.

## ❦ Tough Question

Ted said the toughest question he had to answer his first year in university was "So where are you from?" It made for a great conversation starter, though.

## ❦ Our Kids' Friends

Our boys' friends were always welcome at our house. Whether it was to join us for an hour, a meal, a sleepover, or a cottage stay, the door was always open. Ted and Marshall knew to ask whether someone could stay for dinner, but that was just a formality; we simply needed to know whether to put more pasta in the pot. There were times the four of us would agree to a night in—just family—but other than that, we were always prepared to set another place at the table and pull out the trundle. We tried to make kids feel at home, and apparently we succeeded. By their high school years, some felt comfortable enough to just open the front door, walk in, call out, "Hi, honey, I'm home," then head to the pantry for something from the snack category.

We set limits on behavior. It took awhile for one of Ted's friends to understand that Marshall could not be excluded from activities in his own home, but we sorted that out. There had been the little girl who used to bite Ted, but we sorted that out, too. We came to know and love a lot of kids over the years.

# ❦ No Excuse for Bad Behavior

When things go off the rails and it's time for parental intervention, be sure to label your child's *behavior*, not your child. Don't ever call your kid a #!@ing anything! Don't say, "You are such a dolt."

Kids need you to be clear about what in their behavior was unacceptable. When we saw either of our sons pushing, grabbing, or yelling to get their way, we stepped in and calmly said, "Do not shove or hit. That is the behavior of a bully. If you act like a bully, people will think you *are* a bully, and *no one* likes a bully."

And don't be tricked by the adage "Boys will be boys," which, loosely translated, means someone has given his or her boys permission to be aggressive, mean, disruptive, hurtful, and/or destructive.

The last time I heard the expression was from a father in line at the grocery store. His six-year-old had staged a bit of a tantrum over something desirable that marketers so cleverly place at a six-year-old's eye level. The father had refused to buy whatever it was, so the boy wound up and kicked his father in the shins. The man just shrugged at the stunned onlookers and said, "Boys will be boys."

When *I* think of the phrase "Boys will be boys," here's what I think: Boys will be wonderful. Boys will be captivating. Boys will be funny and athletic and artistic.

Boys will be kind, gentle, competitive, resourceful, perplexing, and thoughtful. Boys will be *terrific*.

That being said, Ted and Marshall loved to wrestle. Whether on the family room rug, in the snow, or on the lawn, they'd often engage in demonstrations of physical strength, both wanting dominance. There was just one rule: "Stop" means stop. It doesn't mean "Maybe I can push this a little further" or "I *will* stop, but not just yet."

Boys need to know that *stop* means stop and *no* means no. They need to develop the self-discipline that is inherent in complying with those directives long before they reach dating age and, as parents, it's our responsibility to ensure they get the message.

## ❦ Honesty versus Discretion

Although I believe we should tell kids the truth about such things as not keeping all their drawings, I don't believe we need to tell children *everything* we know about a topic. Messy details of friends' divorces is a perfect example. What you did in college is another.

## ❦ Controversial Advice

While Ted and Marshall were still youngsters, a colleague gave Steve some advice. We considered it to be good, but others would consider it near blasphemy.

"Don't get your boys involved in hockey," he advised. "Teach them to ski and play golf. Otherwise your whole family is going to be in lockdown for a big part of the year." He meant very cold arenas and early dark mornings—not *my* idea of family fun.

"But if they can ski and golf," he explained, "you can take them on family ski and golf vacations, and they'll *want* to go with you—even when they're teenagers."

That's because teenagers don't have to ski and golf with *you*.

So we didn't tell Marshall or Ted about hockey. Not even how to spell it. We took them to the arena at times when no one was wearing a jersey and taught them how to skate.

They did learn to ski—well, they skied long enough to know they preferred snowboarding—and they learned how to golf. Eventually they found out about hockey, but they have voiced no regrets about missing out on the tryouts and practice schedules. And they do like to come on vacations with us.

Secretly, I was relieved to not be putting them into the hockey culture. Mine was a careful and long-considered opinion, not one held by many in our nation. I just couldn't figure out how I was going to drop our two sweet, young boys off week after week to practice a sport which, if they got *really* good at it and advanced through all the leagues, offered a very good possibility that eventually someone was going to haul off and hit them.

## 🌱 Decorating Kids' Rooms

We've always allowed both Marshall and Ted to have a hand in how their rooms were decorated. Ted chose neon green once. Steve and I pressured him to reconsider and go for a much paler (could I say *saner*?) tint of the swatch he'd fallen in love with. Ted being Ted acquiesced, but Steve and I reconsidered and went ahead with the original choice. It gave Steve headaches.

As both Ted and Marshall got older, I came to understand that a teenage male's approach to décor would always involve something with speakers. In fact, as the sole female in the house, I would know beyond all doubt that someone in my household was exquisitely happy if I came upon (all in one place) speakers, speaker wire, and duct tape.

So the day I returned home to find that Steve and Ted had just mounted black speaker boxes on all four corners of Ted's bedroom walls, I should not have been surprised. But I was, and I made a mistake that day: I told them the speakers had to come down. We were close to putting that house on the market, and, well, I had lots to say about property value and optimizing resale potential and refilling the holes.

They did take them down. They built very handsome speaker stands instead. I thanked them for doing that, but I wasn't happy. I knew I'd spoiled a vision; I'd taken the wind out of Ted's sails and put an end to a father-son project. I should have stepped away and counted to some number probably higher than ten, because a new purchaser could have filled in those holes—right after they'd cleaned under the appliances.

## Very Expensive Maple Syrup

I should have predicted our boys would eventually get around to projects that involved hammers and lumber and sharp tools. After all, I grew up with three younger brothers.

One spring they went out and tapped all the big maple trees that surrounded our large corner property. They poured the sap into an enormous vat and put it on our kitchen stove to boil. Given it takes ten gallons of sap to make one quart of syrup, it meant a lot of boiling. The process created enough sticky vapor that the wallpaper began peeling off the kitchen walls, and that put an end to that.

The next year, with the help of an adult who knew a lot about construction and should have known a lot more about building codes, they built a fort in our backyard. First they cleared a fairly sizable stand of mature lilacs, then they poured a concrete floor. The walls, roof, door, and shutters were constructed out of substantial pieces of evenly sawed boards. They even shingled the roof. Then—get this: they brought power into the shack from a line that somehow tapped directly into the one that supplied electricity from the street to our house. I don't know why they weren't all electrocuted.

So when spring rolled around again, they set another big vat of sap on a two-burner hot plate out in that little sugar shack and boiled it all down to produce one mason jar of syrup, which, based on the electric bill that came to our house later that month, cost about $243.

## ❦ We All Screw Up

We all screw up. I might add that to a family crest. Maybe in Latin.

Here are the three things we told our boys we expected of them when they screwed up (which they did):

1. Admit what you've done—by this we meant *before* somebody finds out what it was.
2. Apologize.
3. Ask what you need to do to set things right.

Our sons got to practice these steps after Sarah Miller got buried in the sand up to her neck and was left for the crows. They had another opportunity after

Aunt Sue's antique oil lamp broke when the sofa cushion hit it. And yet again when somebody experimented with underage drinking and threw up in the back of his history teacher's van.

Unspoken in this approach to restitution is another reason to not hit kids—I know this one from experience. Kids who get hit for screwing up are not necessarily going to change their ways. They may just get really good at lying and covering up what they've done, because more than anything they don't want to get caught. No, actually, more than *anything*, they don't want to get caught because they don't want to get hit again—or yelled at or sworn at—just because they screwed up. Which we all do. Kids who are solely intent on not getting caught may never develop into adults who have the courage to say, "Here's what I did. I'm sorry. What do I need to do to fix this?"

## ⚜️A Family Crest

I got to thinking that a family crest would be a *great* idea. So I imagined one. It's been a terrific exercise, and I recommend it to everyone.

The crest is in the shape of a shield—a symbol of protection, signifying our family's ambition to keep one another safe.

The symbol would also remind me of the Mother's Day I used an open pair of scissors to try to force the small plastic tab on the armband of Marshall's pint-sized, plastic knight's shield back into place. It took four stitches to close the gash in my left thumb. The doctor would have waited for a neurosurgeon to do the job, but this was the day we were all flying to Disney World. Our flight was leaving from the international airport an hour's drive from home, and the whole accident thing had me way behind on my last-minute packing. I told the emergency room doctor about our plans for this midwinter getaway—the sun, the swimming pools, the resort, the water park—and our need to get on our way. So he stitched me up and said only one thing about my thumb before he left: "Keep it dry."

Emblazoned above the shield I'm imagining, in strong, fluid letters is our family name—well, names: Parsons-Jefferies.

Having reached adulthood in the newly forged era of feminism, I had long decided to not change my name when I married, but in addition to that, Steve had been married before—*twice*. And as much as I like the sound of a family crest and its nod to tradition and lineage, I could never get my head around the idea of being Mrs. Stephen Jefferies the Third.

Festooned around the upper edges and the sides of our shield are swags of branches and boughs representing the hours of fun and adventure we have all had outside in the cathedrals of our forests, lakes, and rivers.

The face of my emblem is divided into three fields. The first shows a lengthy path with no clear destination (if you look *really* closely at it, you'll probably see a moving van somewhere off in the distance). On the path are two sets of human footprints, signifying that no one in this family is journeying alone, nor are we ever far from the reach of one who would help if we stumble. Crisscrossing the path and wandering far beyond its borders and back again are the paw prints of a Labrador retriever to remind us there are various routes to get us where we're going.

The second field reveals the images of three things: a lightbulb, a slinky, and a bunch of grapes—emblems of our aspiration to cultivate innovation, flexibility, and a tradition of fun.

The third section of our shield depicts just one thing— an open door—a symbol of refuge and of welcome. It is what we have worked to create wherever we live.

Actually, there wouldn't be three fields, there would be four; the final one would contain the picture of a pencil with the pink nub of an eraser at its end—an acknowledgment that we will make mistakes in this family, but we can always try again.

Scrolled beneath our shield unfurls a banner reading BE THE BEST _____ YOU CAN BE.

It's what we used to tell our sons: Be the best *Ted* you can be. Be the best *Marshall* you can be.

The empty space in the banner is to remind us all of the challenge to fill in the blank and keep trying: Be the best parent you can be. Be the best partner you can be. Be the best friend you can be.

It's not written in Latin, though. It's a hard enough challenge without having to translate it as you go.

# CHAPTER 13

## *It's a Harder Puzzle Than You Think*

I'VE ALWAYS LIKED PUZZLES; SOMETIMES IT JUST TAKES ME AGES TO get the right answer.

As a kid, I was especially intrigued by the riddle about the farmer who had a duck, a bag of corn, and a fox. He needed to take them all to market, and to get there, he had to cross a river in a rowboat. The problem was that the boat would only hold the farmer and one other thing. So the riddle is: How, taking as many trips as necessary, did the farmer get all three things over the river?

He couldn't take the fox first, because the duck would eat the corn in his absence. If he took the corn and left the fox with the duck—well, we all know how that would turn out.

I think the riddle should have been: Why was a farmer taking a fox to market? But that's just me.

Steve's not as keen on puzzlers as I am, but over the years, there's one we've revisited together fairly regularly—the one Dr. Jacono raised when we went for prenatal counseling in his office that day: What is it you can give your kids that *every* kid wants?

What made the puzzle so hard was that Dr. Jacono had already told us the answer: happy parents. But we didn't know what Dr. Jacono *meant*. We knew that if Steve got a golf membership and I got a horse, that would make us happy, but Dr. Jacono had seemed far wiser than that. The more we puzzled over it, and the closer it seemed we should be to the solution, the more elusive the real answer became—the one that would feel like a key in a lock.

It was like that darn farmer quiz. *Obviously*, the farmer should take the duck to the far shore and leave the fox and the corn behind. That has to be the right answer, because foxes don't eat corn. But what next? If, on his second trip, he was to take either the corn *or* the fox, and leave it on the far bank with the duck (in order to row back for the remaining item), things wouldn't go well, which means it can't be the *completely* right answer.

And that's how it seemed to me at times. Dr. Jacono must have been mistaken, because there were days when the term *happy parent* seemed like a complete oxymoron. How are you supposed to be happy when your breasts are leaking milk, when you have to read *Goodnight Moon* yet again, and when given the choice between sex and sleeping, you'd choose sleeping—even if it was in a rowboat with a duck?

But despite not knowing for sure whether we were on the right track, Steve and I forged on.

I don't remember how the weekly tradition got started, but we created Friday night date night. We'd feed Ted and Marshall a simple kids' supper and give them an early bath. Then we'd settle the two of them—no, that's not right, they had their trusty dog, Woody, so that made three of them—upstairs, with the little TV-VCR. Leaving them with the remote control and a snack, Steve and I would head back downstairs and take over the kitchen. We'd open a bottle of wine, turn on some music, light some candles, and start cooking. But maybe we would dance first; anything from the Beach Boys to Dave Matthews. Jive to slow dancing.

I expect the idea stemmed from the reality that dinners out were expensive and so were babysitters. We already had a wonderful kitchen and a family room with a fireplace, so we decided to just "date" at home. Most times, one of us would do all the cooking as a treat for the other. Our house rule on any night was that whoever cooked didn't have to do the dishes, so that evened things out.

We're both good cooks (if you don't include baking), and this was the night we could eat all the things the boys didn't like or weren't ready to try. I craved Steve's famous mussels in lime, cream, and shallot sauce or the rich cioppino he made with crab, whitefish, mussels, and shrimp. Our menus varied, and over the years we experimented with all kinds of new flavors and presentations.

Our boys seemed to understand that this was our sweetheart time, and without our being mean about it, they knew they weren't invited. Our unspoken message was "If there isn't blood involved, don't call us." When the credits rolled at the end of their movie and they'd done an adequate job of brushing their teeth, they would call from the top of the stairs for tuck-in service, and we'd head up to kiss them goodnight. Returning to the dining room table, Steve and I used our time to talk about things that we didn't have time for during our busy week. And we got to finish sentences without being interrupted. We talked about politics and business; movies and books— anything that came to mind.

A lot of our conversation centered on our kids, I know, but rather than focusing on the minutiae of timetables and schedules, here we could ask bigger questions, like whether we were on the right track in our parenting choices. That topic would inevitably bring us back to Dr. Jacono's answer that felt more like a question: How do we give our boys happy parents—take the corn or take the fox?

But sometimes we would address the biggest question of all: How are we doing?

"What do you *mean*, how are we doing?" I had looked blankly at Steve when he first asked me that question, not too long after we started dating.

"I mean how are you and I doing as a couple—getting along and such. How are we *doing*?"

He might as well have asked me how much I weighed. *Nobody* I'd ever known talked about those things. They all just went along blindly in their relationships, till they either arrived at a happy destination or fell off the cliff. But that's the kind of thing Steve and I would talk about.

So when Uncle Dave came to live with us (along with his dog, Suzie), we set another place at the table and invited him to join in. My youngest brother's marriage had ended in a fairly spectacular fashion. He needed a place to live until he got back on his feet, and we had room. He volunteered to make himself scarce on Friday nights, but he was family, and we thought he could do with some good food and some good talks.

I guess he thought so, too. He liked the camaraderie, the mussels, and the chance to talk about things like "How are we doing?" In fact, after a couple of months of living with us, Dave admitted that he'd been fibbing to his coworkers at the office every Friday.

"Come out with us," his buddies kept urging. They knew he was living the single life again and were no doubt trying their best to cheer him up. Rather than slight them or their good intentions, Dave would keep his preference of spending the evening with Steve and me a secret by simply telling them, "I'd really like to, but

I can't. My sister expects me home on Fridays." As if.

Dave lived with us for close to a year. We had many Friday nights together. It was a great time for all of us to talk and test our theories on love, friendship, and family; a time to learn from one another; a time to consider the happy parent conundrum.

After Dave moved out, Steve and I decided to expand on the success of our Friday night date nights and take our first sweetheart holiday. We hired our dear friend Fran to stay with the boys. I wrote out the whole long list of after-school activities, meal ideas and bedtime rituals, emergency contact phone numbers, when to feed the dog, who our dentist was and how to operate the TV (including diagrams of the various remote controls and little arrows to the corresponding buttons). Then Steve and I headed off to Florida for some precious time together.

That holiday gave us the chance to reconnect and recharge. We walked the beach and sat by the pool. We dined out and rode our bikes to breakfast every day. We got to look each other in the eye as we listened. We touched. We made good use of our moonlit balcony. And, as always, we talked.

It was such a success that we did it again the next year and the next. For close to two decades, we've done this. Twice we took Ted and Marshall along with us, but they never expected to be included, and, in fact, I think our leaving gave them a refreshing break from us. While we were gone, they got to eat loaves of soft white Italian bread, exalt in Fran's sloppy joes, and learn how to play pinochle. As the years passed, they took over looking after themselves and Woody. I doubt they ever consulted the lists I left of meal ideas, emergency contacts, or the phone number for our dentist, but it seems they fed the dog.

Each year, when family camp at Wabanaki rolled around, Steve and I followed another tradition: we would leave the crowd of parents and kids on the beach and head out over the bridge to the deserted island. I know what the others thought we were up to, but they were wrong. We headed, each time, to the same soft-shouldered outcropping of granite that sloped down and disappeared into the green water, and we sat in the sun and talked about how we were doing. It became known as our Talk on the Rock.

Looking back, I recognize there were some unspoken rules in that sanctuary under the open sky: no threats, no stockpiling grievances, and no blaming. At times, it felt that we were risking everything, finding the courage to say things like "This isn't good enough. I need it to be better. I *want* it to be better." They were scary words to speak and often more difficult to hear, but each time we stood up from those rocks to rejoin our friends on the beach, it was with a renewed sense of each other's love and commitment.

Given that the Talk on the Rock covered our needs, Steve and I dealt with our dreams differently. Every few years, often on a Friday night, we'd sit with pencils and notepad, or markers and chart paper, and make a list of what we'd like to do that we hadn't done yet. Our list ranged from the practical through the seemingly improbable, and sometimes was color-coded: lose ten pounds, visit Easter Island, get a puppy. Make a second baby. Write a book.

We have all those sheets of paper in a folder. We take them out every now and then and marvel at how many goals and dreams we've actually achieved and at how many more we would like to achieve.

Each of these rituals we had created felt like a piece of the solution to our good doctor's puzzle. We were trying lots of things in order to be happy parents, but the sum of our efforts seemed to fall uncomfortably short of what I imagined to be his benevolent scrutiny. Gourmet dinners, trips to Florida, unfettered time at camp—they all seemed too self-centered and too self-absorbed to be the *right* answer.

I was always a little fearful that if I took my eye off the puzzle for too long, I'd do a wrong thing. Steve and I could become *unhappy* parents. The fox would eat the duck.

So it's kind of funny how it came to me on a Friday night in mid-August when Steve and I were out on the deck overlooking the forest. We were having a glass of wine before dinner and watching to see if deer might wander through the woods. Ted and Marshall were home briefly from their summer jobs as greens keepers at a golf resort a two-hour drive away. They were working to sock away spending money for the upcoming university year. They had a couple of days off, and they'd decided to come home, eat well, sleep late, and do laundry for free. A lot of laundry.

Their jobs entailed getting up at five o'clock every morning to be out on the course—rain or shine—with mowers and rakes and other tools of the trade. They would have had to pay to ride the resort shuttle to work each morning, but as their year-end gift I had given them the use of my station wagon for the summer; so they took turns driving to the implement shed just as the sun began to rise. Once there, they rode the tractors and worked side by side from dawn till midafternoon. Then they had free time to golf, fish, swim, play guitar, write songs, and rest up after the Tuesday night bus trip to and from a distant resort that hosted a weekly concert (well, more like a party). All the neighboring resorts' staff members were invited.

For accommodations, Marshall and Ted shared a room in a defunct motel the golf resort had purchased to provide housing for its out-of-town employees. It reminded me a lot of the Primrose Motel, with its compact little bathroom, window air conditioner, smallish closet, and two twin beds—except this room had a beer fridge. Actually, it had two fridges. One was supposed to be for food, but *that* one didn't seem to work very well, and given the choice between cold food and cold beer, the boys opted to keep their beer close and their edible provisions in the communal kitchen at the end of the complex. Together they decided on menus, shopped for groceries, and cooked dinners. Then they packed enormous lunches from the leftovers to fuel their bodies for the next day's work.

When they could coordinate their days off, they would hop in the little Ford station wagon and drive an hour north to hang out with their friends, Brian and Kevin, who'd gone back to Wabanaki for yet another summer of camp employment.

Our sons were in each other's company pretty much *all* the time.

"Do you ever fight?" I asked them on that Friday night in mid-August, while we were all sitting around on the deck. They had both taken much-needed showers (with no apparent dispute over who got to go first), and then they had joined us on the deck to share appetizers, stories, and great golf jokes.

"No." Ted looked surprised at my question.

"Argue?" I prodded.

Marshall appeared to think back quickly over their months together. "Nope," he said.

"Do you ever even get on each other's nerves?"

Marshall shrugged and mimicked Ted's wagging head. "Nope."

A little while later, after Ted and Marshall had retreated to the cool of the basement to play video games before dinner, Steve and I listened to their sounds coming from the rec room: two young men yacking away, then hoots of laughter, and back to the chatter.

"I don't get it," I said, turning to Steve. "They spend all day and all night together. They are *never* apart. What do they still have to talk about?"

In the silence before Steve could answer, I got a thin edge of the wedge of insight. Our sons had probably been asking each other *exactly* the same question about *us* for years. I could just *hear* them: "Dad and Mom are *always* together. What do they still have to *talk* about?"

Then a broader understanding hit me—something that had eluded me since that day in the doctor's office—and finally I understood what Dr. Jacono had meant.

As a girl, I never knew what would greet me when I pushed open the door to the home where I grew up. My parents could be cuddling on the sofa, or there could be yelling, hitting, and crying. There might be dancing beside the hi-fi record player or plates of food being thrown. I never knew.

It had taken me a long time to figure this puzzle out, but at last I had the right answer.

Kids want to walk in the door—every day, every time—to a home in which their parents demonstrate love, kindness, and commitment to each other. Children who witness such stand-alone strength in their parents' relationship feel safe and secure. They are free to pursue their *own* happiness, intrinsically knowing they are not responsible for their parents' joy, and they have a wonderful model from which to begin.

Over the years, without really knowing what we were doing, Steve and I had managed to give our sons what every kid wants: happy parents.

## ❦ The Wonderful Adventure of Parenting

When I married at the age of thirty-five, I didn't change my surname. In jest, within our sons' earshot, I have said that Steve and I knew we wanted kids and I figured that this way, if the children didn't turn out well, I could always say I was only related to them through marriage.

When we were ready to start a family, Steve and I decided that we wanted a stay-at-home parent and that it would be me. Steve's earning potential was greater than mine at the time. He had spent years climbing the corporate ladder, and we were enjoying his level of success. I had worked many years as an elementary school teacher and then in the advertising business. Now I was excited about the challenge of figuring out how to be both *me* and *Mom* and not only stay sane but have fun.

So I stayed home, and I had fun. I made mistakes and I'll probably make more still, but I have tried to be the best parent, the best mom, I could be. I used to peer into our sons' faces and wonder, "Who are you?" But now I know. As they have matured, their distinct characters—their true natures—have been revealed to those who have been paying attention. They know themselves so well they've made it easy for us to know them, too.

I am grateful we have been able to do what we hoped to do as a family. I am thankful beyond words for our family's health. Parenting has been a wonderful adventure.

## All for One and One for All

While our boys were still very little, Steve and I came to the conclusion that it was time for Steve to realize his dream of working independently as a consultant. That choice has reaped many rewards and a number of challenges. It also gave us the freedom to move a lot.

Generally, when people asked me what *I* did for a living, I told them I put things away. But along with that, I found various means over the years of contributing to our family income: telemarketing for an interior design company; providing after-school care for a neighbor's son; working as a home stager, preparing houses for the real estate market—all things I could organize around our family's schedule. No matter where the money came from, how much it was, or who earned it, Steve and I held to the same agreement we've had from the beginning: it's all *our* money.

## Time Together at Little Cost

Finding time to be together as a couple without it being expensive was tricky. Having a dog that re-

quired walking twice a day, regardless of the weather (remember, Woody was from Labrador, and I don't think you get to make any excuses to *anyone* from Labrador for not going outside), gave us an idea.

We hired Laurie, a lovely high school girl from up the street. We put her on retainer, actually. At the beginning of every month, we paid Laurie forty bucks. The deal was that she would come to our house every Tuesday and Thursday, *after* the boys were tucked in, and sit while Steve and I took Woody out for about forty minutes. She didn't have to *do* anything, since the boys were in bed and stayed there, so she got her homework done, Steve and I got time together, Woody got his walk, and Laurie got paid even if we canceled on her because someone was throwing up.

## Gifts in Our Absence

When Steve and I were heading away on a sweetheart holiday and Ted and Marshall were still young, we dulled any anxiety they might feel about our departure by leaving a pile of small wrapped gifts for them to open in our absence—one per day per kid. On the tags were their names and the days on which the presents were to be opened. That way, the boys would have some sense of when Dad and Mom were coming home: the smaller the pile, the closer the day of return—which, when I think of it, may have created a sense of

disappointment that we were coming home at all.

The biggest gift ever would have been a newly released movie. Knowing the boys would watch it many times over in a week (and it would thus also be a gift to Fran), it would have been marked to open the first day. Other than that, the gifts were simple little things like a box of M&Ms, mini-Lego sets, or KinderSurprise, chocolate eggs with miniature toys inside.

## What is Marriage?

There is a definition of marriage I really like: Marriage is the commitment to be witness to someone else's life.

It is not my job (despite many misguided and hence unsuccessful attempts) to get Steve to cooperate. My commitment is to do the best I can to let him grow. In return, I'm afforded exactly the same sweet, difficult opportunity in life.

## Marriage as a Separate Entity

I think of marriage as a third presence in the room, always—an entity that is separate from both Steve and me but resides with us, invisible and silent. The thing about marriage is that while it is both strong and resilient, it is utterly fragile. It can be fortified and made more robust with patience, humor, and affection. And just as easily, it can be wounded and made unstable by derision or neglect.

Marriage is not self-sustaining, I remind myself. It cannot feed itself, so there exists a real threat that without nurturing, it could wither, fade, and die. Thus, in the choices I make, I try to remember this: do good things for myself, do good things for Steve, and do good things for our marriage. It is profoundly important to me.

Steve is the best thing that ever came into my life—a good enough reason for you to encourage those you know to go on blind dates.

## Fighting Words

Don't be fooled. Steve and I have had some humdinger fights in our time. Like the rest of the population, I don't think well when I'm angry, so holding fast to this vague sense of our marriage watching from the sidelines, wondering whether it will survive, has helped keep me from destroying it with words I can't retract.

## Getting Engaged

If I were in charge of naming things, there are two I would reverse: being *engaged* and being *married*. The way things are right now, couples consider themselves engaged for a short time and married for some yet-to-be-determined period.

Wouldn't we do better as couples if we worked on staying engaged *after* we got married?

## ᨀ The Answer to the Riddle

Take the duck. Leave it on the far shore. Go back for the fox. Drop off the fox, but pick up the duck and take it back with you in the boat. Leave the duck alone on the riverbank and take the corn. Leave the corn with the fox and go back for the duck.

Like the mystery of how to become happy parents, there may be other answers to this riddle. If I had been less worried about finding the *right* answer I might have thought to expand on one solution for this brainteaser that I found online: set the fox free, have grilled duck and roasted corn on the riverbank with Steve, and make love in the rowboat.

## ᨀ One More Thing

There are many responsibilities to be taken on as a parent. Perhaps I could be allowed to add yet another to the list, *one more thing* to be done each and every day without fail. I hope it will take priority over many, many other duties and still be one of the easiest and most joyous in any parent's day.

Catch your child doing something good.

# Acknowledgments

I WOULD LIKE TO THANK: Stephanie Riddell for asking lots of questions and laughing at my answers. Carrie Anderson for falling in love with our dog and inspiring me to write this book. Jen Cook (who still has her gingham apron, by the way) for telling me to keep writing. Dona Harvey for being embedded in my life. Willy and Vi Hayden for a place at their table where I learned the right way to do some important things and that buttering a slice of bread can be an art form. Deb Woeller who despite her instructive mantra: NOT MY KID, NOT MY PROBLEM continues to care for kids wherever she goes.

Everyone who is, was, or will be a camp counselor or a teacher, for investing in children's lives.

Steve, Ted, and Marshall for an unending source of rich material and years of joy and laughter.

Thank you to Peter Vegso and everyone at HCI Books for the chance to cross one more thing off my bucket list. Ian Briggs, my editor, for always playing by rule number three: Have Fun.

And the Universe: thank you for listening.